JPL
BOOKS

PRICE, $ELL, PRODUCE!

Can you dig it?

Price, $ell, Produce!
Can you dig it?
by J. Paul Lamarche

Contact: JPL Consulting, 236 Millard Avenue,
Newmarket, Ontario, Canada L3Y 1Z2
Telephone: 416-606-9124 or Email: sales@jplbiz.ca

For a complete listing of JPL publications, please visit www.jplbiz.ca

ISBN 978-1-897528-39-6
PUBLISHED BY JPL BOOKS
236 MILLARD AVENUE NEWMARKET, ONTARIO L3Y 1Z2

JPL Consulting
Exceeding expectations since 1984

TABLE OF CONTENTS

CHAPTER 1

PRODUCTIVITY AND ITS EFFECT ON OVERHEAD

1.1 VEHICLE PRODUCTIVITY

After many seasons of seminars, workshops and one-to-one consulting, and especially after numerous discussions with landscaping companies, I have learned that average company overheads have increased over the years. I believe that higher overheads are due to:

- Extremely low pricing based on the premise that volume sales are more profitable.
- Poor productivity due to poor pricing, poor training and poor wages.
- Poor judgment regarding choice of equipment and vehicles.

These are concerns I would like to address in my book.

A benchmark overhead for a landscaping company is 32%, including ROI[1] (return on investment for vehicles and equipment.) The reality however is quite different, as the average overhead in landscaping is about 40%.

This figure is eight points above the benchmark and represents quite a substantial difference. Does this mean that landscaping companies are out on a spending spree? This is definitely not the case, based on the financial data I have examined. Almost all the companies I observed during this time seem to be suffering from this same high overhead problem. What is the reason for this high overhead?

Perhaps we should be phrasing the question a little differently and take into account how many *production* vehicles a landscaping company owns.

---

[1] This is included in your overhead.

The question then becomes: How much *productivity* is it possible to generate using one production vehicle and a crew of three?

We should then also ask: How high is the overhead for each vehicle? When we ask these questions, it soon becomes apparent that excessive overhead is not so much a problem of overspending as a problem of inadequate productivity combined with improper job site direction.

Let me ask the question again. How much revenue can be generated with one production vehicle? In the North American market, where there are as many as 35 possible weeks of productivity, one vehicle operating at 100% capacity with a crew of three properly trained employees should generate between $3,000 (low) and $8,000 (high) per day.

FACTORS THAT INFLUENCE OVERHEAD
Poor pricing strategies
Job takes longer to complete than originally forecast
Poor equipment
Vehicles with less than adequate productivity
Combination of the above

1.2 HOW MUCH REVENUE CAN BE GENERATED?

How much revenue *can* be generated with just one vehicle? Here are some interesting benchmarks.

- Many companies generate only $2,000 per day per vehicle or less.
- A vehicle that generates $2,000 per day for 5 days x 35 weeks will bring in revenue of $350,000.
- A vehicle bringing in $3,000 per day x 5 days x 35 weeks will result in revenue of $525,000.
- For a company generating $1 million in net sales[2], $320,000 overhead per year[3] translates into $2,133.34 overhead per day.

In my own particular case, our landscaping division consistently generates over $5,000 per day[4]. The $5,000 per day generated requires only one truck, and two employees. No other equipment, trailers or excavators are required.

What does $5,000 per day x 35 weeks amount to? If we calculate $5,000 per day x one truck x 5 days x 35 weeks this would equal $875,000 in revenue.

TO INCREASE REVENUE
Improve pricing strategy by improving selling strategy
Increase productivity (crews, equipment and vehicles)
Optimize profit
Maintain a good reputation

---

2 Net sales = Gross sales less sales tax, less all subcontractor costs.
3 Benchmark overhead of 32%.
4 This division specializes in planting jobs that average $5,000 per day.

FIG. 1.1 REVENUE GENERATED WITH ONE TRUCK

REVENUE/DAY	DAYS/WEEK	TOTAL WEEKS	REVENUE/YEAR
$2000	5	35	$350,000
$3000	5	35	$525,000
$5000	5	35	$875,000

For a company generating $1 million this means:

- **$320,000 overhead per year OR**
- **$2,133.34 overhead per day, per vehicle**
- **Benchmark overhead is 32%**

1.3 INCREASING PRODUCTIVITY

Equipment and vehicles are an important component of overhead. For example, a landscaping company that generates $1 million in sales and has a benchmark overhead of 32% has an actual overhead of $320,000. This $320,000 yearly overhead translates into $2,133.34 overhead per day, per vehicle, based on working 5 days per week x 35 weeks. It should be possible to generate over $1 million in landscaping sales from two fully-equipped vehicles.[5]

If this company requires three vehicles to produce the same revenue, then the overhead obviously increases beyond 32% due to increased gas expense, repairs, insurance and other related costs. Unchecked, overhead can easily reach 40% and higher.

How does high overhead adversely affect profitability? To be competitive in pricing, the combination of overhead percentage and desired profit percentage should not exceed 50% of net sales.

---

[5] Based on $3,000 per day per day per vehicle.

1.4 COMPETITIVE PRICING AND PAYING EMPLOYEES PROPERLY

To compete effectively today, you have to aim at increasing the productivity of your company. When productivity is high, it is much easier to price competitively. This is because your overhead as a percentage of sales decreases.

For example, you can do more jobs if you produce $5,000 per day vs. $2,000 per day. Attaining $5,000 per day is possible with programmed productivity, proper pricing and strategic selling.

To attain a high level of productivity, your company must have well-trained employees. It follows that if you want to retain good employees, you must pay them adequately. It is quite possible to pay landscaping employees $25 to $30 per hour if they are part of a productive crew, working in a company that has a 32% overhead and produces $5,000 in sales per day.

Look at Fig. 1.2. Three employees in one vehicle, earning a combined wage average of $25 per hour plus employee benefits of 20% would translate into the following labour costs.

- $90 per hour for the 3 employees x 12 hours or $1,080.
- $1,080 in labour costs ÷ $5,000 daily sales = 21.6%
- Benchmark employee payroll as a percentage of net sales is 25%

FIG. 1.2 LABOUR COSTS

COST PER HOUR	# OF EMPLOYEES	# OF HOURS	LABOUR COST	LABOUR COST %
$90	3	12	$1,080	21.6%

Look at the labour cost percentage. In this example, $1,080 in labour costs divided by daily sales of $5,000 would work out to 21.6%. Labour costs below 25% are considered excellent.

What does an employee earn for your company? For an employee earning $30 per hour, calculate as shown in Fig. 1.3.

FIG. 1.3 WHAT AN EMPLOYEE EARNS FOR YOUR COMPANY

<u>$30.00 per hour (benefits included)</u>
100% - 32% overhead

= $44.12 per hour

Using the $44.12 per hour as an example, how would annual revenue and labour costs look? An employee earning $44.12 per hour for your company will generate $77,210 in labour sales. If three employees generate $3,000 per day, this adds up to $525,000 in sales per year. Look at Fig. 1.4.

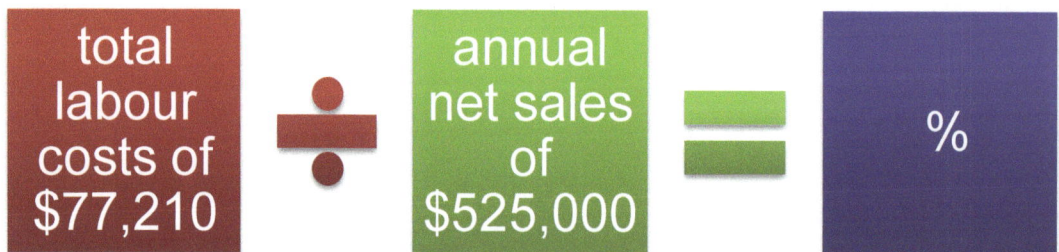

| total labour costs of $77,210 | ÷ | annual net sales of $525,000 | = | % |

P R I C E , $ E L L ,   P R O D U C E   …   C A N   Y O U   D I G   I T ?

10

FIG. 1.4 REVENUE AND LABOUR COSTS[6]

- An employee earning $44.12 per hour for your company x 5 days per week x 10 hours x 35 weeks at break-even will generate $77,210 in labour sales.

- Three employees generating $3,000 per day x 5 days per week x 35 weeks, adds up to $525,000 in sales per year.

- Labour at 25% adds up to $131,250 or $43,750 per employee.

- $43,750 ÷ $30 per hour = 1,458 hours.

- Balance of sales/expenses = material expense, equipment/vehicles expense, and profit.

1.6 WORKING SMARTER, WORKING PRODUCTIVELY

Landscaping is a creative merging of craft and design. A landscape designer's imagination is limited only by the availability of materials, employee craftsmanship and the financial resources of the customer paying for the work.

PRODUCTIVE CREW = GOOD RENUMERATION

Productive employees can be paid $25 - $30 per hour.

In a productive company overhead is about 32%.

In a productive company, labour is 25% of daily sales.

In a productive company, good employees are retained.

A well-organized landscaping company manages its employees with the same care that is given to the estimating and design process.

---

[6] These figures are very significant.

To increase productivity, employees must be trained to be accountable and to work "smarter." Unfortunately, nine out of ten companies send out their landscaping crews to new jobs with only minimal instruction. This is a recipe for disaster. The fastest way to frustrate employees is to send them out to cut down a tree with an unsharpened axe!

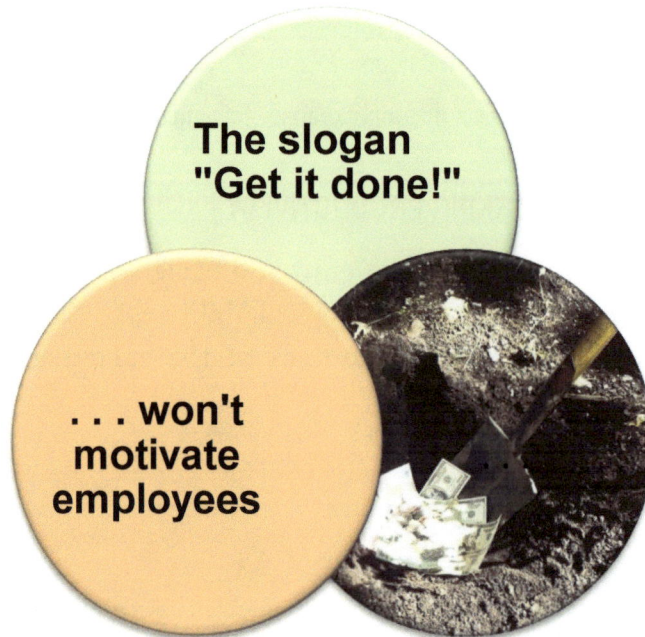

1.7 MANAGEMENT TOOL

There is an easy solution that requires only a minimum investment of time. Using a simple, well-planned form could do much to prevent potential problems or misunderstandings.

The simple management tool shown in Fig. 1.5 measures productivity and is easy to use.

(FIG. 1.5) MEASURING PRODUCTIVITY (SAMPLE FORM)

JOB: Mr. & Mrs. Smith   Date:

ADDRESS:

TASKS FOR JOB	ESTIMATED TIME REQUIRED	ACTUAL TIME REQUIRED

COMMENTS:
Why did this job take more/less time to complete?

What could have been done to improve productivity?

Site Supervisor:	Designer:
Date:	Estimator:

P R I C E , $ E L L ,   P R O D U C E   ...   C A N   Y O U   D I G   I T ?

• • •
13

HOW THE TOOL WORKS

- The designer or employee responsible for a particular design lists each major task associated with the job and the estimated time to complete this task.
- In this system, site supervisors are responsible for entering the actual time that was required to complete the job.
- Site supervisors add comments regarding why a particular job task took more or less than the estimated time.

This simple management tool can provide owners and managers with valuable information for evaluating productivity. It also puts the onus on employees to be responsible time-managers and allows them to more actively participate in the organization of their company.

This is a win-win situation. Responsible, conscientious workers are valuable assets to a landscaping company because they reduce overhead and generate higher profits. Companies that think long term, in turn, should have no problem paying such employees higher wages.

TO PREVENT MISUNDERSTANDINGS

include everyone involved in project management . . .

1. estimator
2. designer
3. site supervisor

CHAPTER 2

THE REAL ART OF SELLING: THERE IS A TEMPLATE

2.1 EVERYONE CAN SELL

Salespeople are a dime a dozen. Everyone can sell. In fact, most people *think* they can sell. Are these statements true? No.

It doesn't really matter *what* you sell, but to be successful in sales, the essential ingredients are always the same. You must:

- Really know your product
- Position yourself in the marketplace
- Promote opportunities
- Have an abundance of ideas and enthusiasm
- Sell your price, don't price to sell
- Know about and believe in "service, service, service"

2.2 REALLY KNOW YOUR PRODUCT

A truly beautiful landscape consists of *hardscaping* and *softscaping*. Proficiency in *hardscaping* is not as complex as becoming proficient in *softscaping,* as there is a limited selection of hardscaping products. *Softscaping,* on the other hand, is more difficult, as there are approximately 10,000 different plants to choose from. *Softscaping* colours, softens and complements the *hardscape.*

Knowing your plants and their characteristics will make a big difference in your presentation. Do your research and expand your knowledge on a continual basis.

2.3 POSITIONING YOURSELF IN THE MARKETPLACE

All jobs can be successful and profitable, but if you want to maximize your profits, you need to attract a specific clientele and type of work. The most sought-after work is for clientele who require an actual plan. The requirement for a precise plan indicates a commitment to quality, attention to detail and understanding that landscaping is an investment.

Think of a sales presentation as your opportunity to excel. Your product knowledge and your design ideas will separate you from your competitors. Remember, you are selling your price, your ideas and your services. Live up to your reputation. Exceed customer expectations.

2.4 PROMOTE OPPORTUNITIES

Did you know that 82% percent of landscaping work comes from recommendations? You need to promote opportunities so that you can meet your target clientele. Where is the best place to meet these people? Think about their business environments. Think about their recreational preferences.

Promoting yourself means physically getting out there and letting yourself be seen. Join clubs and network with key people who offer you the likelihood of meeting your preferred clientele. Of course, this is quite an investment of your time, but if you handle this well, you will reap the rewards.

Promote opportunities → by networking in person

2.5 ARE YOU PERCEIVED TO BE TOO EXPENSIVE?

Ask yourself this question, "Why are some contractors able to ask for $75 per hour and receive this from their customers while others have difficulty asking for $25 per hour?"

It is quite customary for a customer to ask, "Are you expensive?" My answer to this question is, *"I deliver exactly what I have promised you. You are investing in my company, my knowledge, my employees, as well as your home. I am considered to be of the best in this field, and that's why you invited me here. Your return on investment is most important to our company."*

2.6 YOUR ONLY COMPETITOR

Your number one competitor is yourself. If the customer chooses not to engage your services, move on and console yourself with the thought that this might simply be an indication that you are recognized as the best and this customer cannot afford to hire you *at this time*. Accept this gracefully, with the realization that this same customer may call you two years later and surprise you by saying, "I'm ready to hire you now!"

You only have one REAL competitor.

That competitor is YOU!

2.7 IDEAS AND ENTHUSIASM

Separate yourself immediately from the competition. Are you aware that approximately 80% of contractors simply ask what the customer wants and then merely deliver accordingly? This is their preferred way of doing business because there is no need to "put their neck on the block." They avoid risk and potential trouble spots, but they miss out on many opportunities.

The other 20% of contractors also ask what the customer wants, but they maximize the potential in a sales presentation by offering their own ideas as well. Show your customer that you care about your work and are willing to explore various possibilities and approaches. You never know where these ideas may lead. They just might stimulate your customer into hiring you for more landscaping work than was originally intended.

Allow me to illustrate with a personal example. A customer called me for an estimate because he needed help with sprucing up the yard and setting up a dog run. During the conversation, I found out he was planning to move to a larger property so that he could have a pool installed.

Directly off the house, the existing backyard was actually quite small. But the side yard was quite large. I asked, "How about if we punch a hole in the side wall of the house and install a pool in the side yard?" This possibility had never crossed my customer's mind until that moment. To make a long story short, a small job became a very large job, and I actually won an award for this job.

2.8 THINK FURTHER

To gain access to larger and/or more lucrative jobs, you must be armed with ideas that inspire and stimulate customers to think further than the obvious. Otherwise, you are only going to attract those jobs that are limited to "apple to apple" comparisons.

When "lowest price" plays the dominant role, customers merely select the lowest price, based on their needs. Your selling success rate will always be better than 80% *if you sell "idea" before "price."*

Don't be afraid to explore other possibilities!

2.9 SERVICE, SERVICE, SERVICE

It is important that you are just as approachable and accessible to your customer now as you were during the sales presentation. How does a company treat a customer when service is required? That is the real test of quality!

If you offer a top-notch after-sales service, half the work of obtaining referrals is already done. If you do good work and offer good after-sales service, customers will always recommend you to their friends and families.

What does "service" mean in plain language? Below are my company service policies and these policies apply to *all* my customers.

- Here is my personal cellphone number; please call me if the need arises.
- All my calls or emails are returned within 24 hours.
- All callbacks or replacements will be handled within 3 days of notification.
- Please call me in the spring, to let me know how your landscaping looks after the winter and/or to discuss any concerns or questions you may have.

CHAPTER 3

WINNING 8 OUT OF 10 SALES = TIME MANAGEMENT

3.1 FIND YOUR OWN STYLE

Try to find your own style. There are probably over a million selling techniques. Talk to everyone who knows you. Find out what is special about you. Find out what you can improve on. Collect selling tips.

In my own experience, I have seen a wide variety of people with excellent sales ability. They may be short, tall, skinny, chubby, talkative, reticent, well-dressed, sloppy, well-groomed or not groomed at all. There are as many adjectives to describe salespeople as there are sales techniques. These people may show up in fancy SUVs, *Smart* cars, old trucks or in cars held together with tape.

Find your own style and make it work for you. Incorporate the tips in this booklet into your sales presentation, and you will be a very busy and highly recommended contractor, provided that you live up to your sales presentation.

Remember that the most valued sales ingredient is *trust*. The most successful salespeople build trust throughout the sales presentation and their relationship with the customer.

| Find your own selling style. | → | Don't try to imitate other salespeople. |

3.2 PROJECTING THE RIGHT IMAGE

To "sell" your company, let your customer know about its outstanding features:

- If you are a family business, it is important that you emphasize this feature! Example: add "family-owned and operated" or "privileged to have served this community since ...." on all your promotional material.
- State the number of years in service.
- Inform the customer of your area of specialization.
- List previous customers you have worked for.
- Give references if possible. Remember that big talkers are a dime a dozen. References are priceless.
- List any awards you have won. Use photos.
- List any associations to which your company belongs.
- List any community events that you sponsor.
- Elaborate on the kind of employees you have, the training you provide, the pride you have in their workmanship.
- List the type of equipment you use.
- Explain the guarantee that you offer.
- Explain the kind of insurance you have, i.e., Workplace Safety and Insurance Board, Professional Liability, Bonding, Construction Lien Act. Offer to leave a copy for the customer.

3.3 SELL YOUR PRICE, DON'T "PRICE TO SELL"

Know your break-even price. Once you have established your break-even price, you have the power of this knowledge behind you. No guessing or wondering about pricing your job. You will get your price, *if you know your price.* If the market will "bear" more, this is up to you.

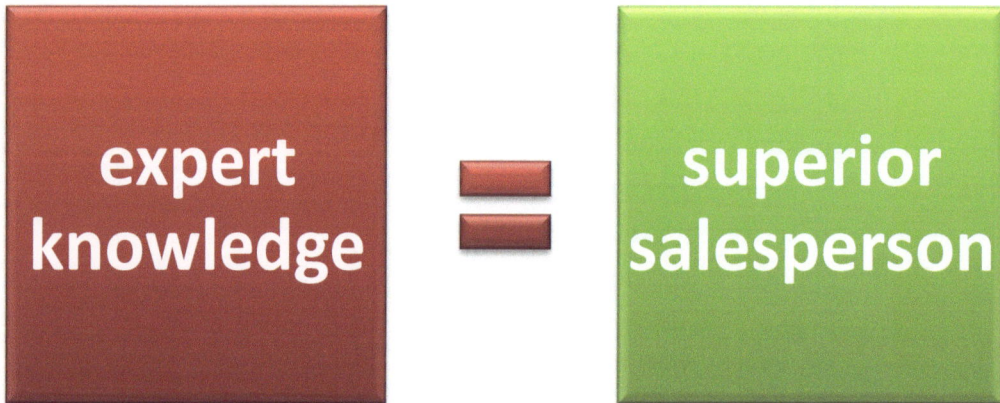

expert knowledge = **superior salesperson**

3.4 THE CONSULTATION

Did you bring everything you need for the consultation? Here are some examples of what you should be taking along when you visit your customer.

- Freebies, i.e., a pack of seeds, a plant or a seedling, tickets to a garden show
- Business card
- Business pamphlet
- Photo album
- Plant book, photo book, catalogues on plant material
- List of references, testimonials from customers
- Samples of products to be used, i.e. paving stones or flagstones
- Letter of good standing from Workplace Safety and Insurance Board
- Copy of company guarantee
- Date book for next appointment

I was often asked for a discount. My solution was to say to the customer: *Let's start this presentation over again at the door. When I come in again, I will offer you a 10% discount.*

This worked every time!

3.5 BUILDING CREDIBILITY

- Project a positive image of your company.
- Let your customer know how you may be contacted.
- Call ahead to confirm dates or inform the customer of delays.
- Ask if the customer can be on site during the job.
- Provide progress reports.
- Admit errors and fix them.
- Leave written instructions on how to maintain the landscape.
- Show your customer the technical points of the landscape construction and how these may be of benefit.
- Never "bad mouth" anyone for any reason. NEVER "bad mouth" your competitors.

Ensure that ALL parties involved in the sale are present for ALL meetings.

3.6 LISTEN TO YOUR CUSTOMER

Are you listening to your customer? Body language speaks volumes. Here are some examples.

- Make eye contact.
- No nervous movement or fidgeting. Your body language may say more about you than you want to reveal.
- Smile and nod in agreement when appropriate.
- Probing (expanding on certain important points).
- Ask questions, take notes on your customer's ideas.
- Answer all concerns, especially your customer's worries. Ease all their fears. Examples: We will finish on time, we will stay within the budget, we will meet or exceed your expectations, I will be on the job every day, we will work with your neighbours, we tidy up every day as well as when the job is completed.
- Offer to give the customer your own cellphone number.
- Give positive feedback.
- Set up another appointment immediately so that you can present the drawing and/or contract.

3.7 HOW TO RUIN A SALES PRESENTATION

Doing the following will *not* win you eight out of ten sales.

- Showing up late. You should always call, even if you will only be a few minutes late.
- Showing up unshaven, messy.
- Showing up without your business card.
- Showing up without your company pamphlet.
- Refusing to go inside the house or spend extra time.
- Asking customers how much they want to spend. Do they have a budget?
- Not prepared to offer ideas.
- Not prepared with product information.
- Not showing enthusiasm.
- Not "connecting" with your customer. Learn how to break the ice.
- "Badmouthing" competitors.
- Not paying attention to your customer's needs, ideas and concerns.
- Taking a long time to get back to your customer with the design or quote.

3.8 QUESTIONS TO ASK

There are certain questions that you may want to ask your customer to facilitate the consultation process and to ensure that you have all the details you require to create your design.

Questions should be pertinent to the job.

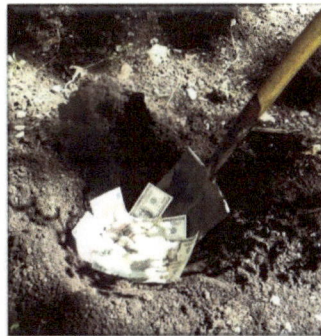

Here are some samples of pertinent questions.

- Is this your first home?
- Will you be moving in the near future?
- How do you visualize the landscape?
- Do you have specific ideas about landscaping?
- How would you like to use your backyard?
- Do you like having flowers all season long?
- Do you want your landscape to be "maintenance free"?
- Do you have pets?
- Do you entertain outdoors?
- Do you want a vegetable garden?
- Do you want to attract birds?
- Do you like cut flowers?
- Do you like to garden?

There are many ways to ask these types of questions. Make sure you get all the information you need.

3.9 NEGATIVE PERCEPTIONS

Be aware that your customer may have negative perceptions about you and/or your industry. You will have to try to overcome these. Try to focus on the positive and think about the following.

- If you make a promise, keep it!
- If you knock down other people or companies, your customer may think that *you* are hiding something. This is one of the worst things you can do.
- Critical remarks about *another* customer will make *this* customer worry.
- Nothing is free. Thank your customer for asking and let them down easy.

- Don't "bite the hand that feeds you" because if you lose your customer's confidence, you will lose the job.
- Dress for the occasion.
- Lack of enthusiasm will translate into lack of interest in the customer.
- You know the product, so tell the customer about it.
- "No one has good service anymore." Prove to your customer that this is not true. Tell them what you will do to alleviate their concerns.
- "Young people don't know very much." Show your customer that though you may be young, you are well informed, you have an excellent reputation and you want this job.

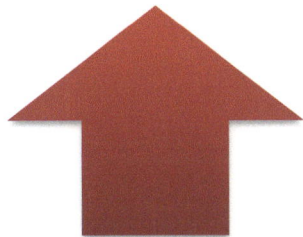

always focus
on the positive!

3.10 WHAT FEATURES ARE YOU SELLING?

No one knows the features of your design better than you do. If you want to win eight out of ten sales, you must try to convey these features to your customer. Knowledge is power, and you have the power to make your design come alive.

Expand on the highlights. Know your material, especially when it comes to plants and colours. You should be able to expand on any plant or product to bring your design to life.

Here are some examples of particular plants and their special features.

Golden Elf Spirea

- Naturally slow-growing and exceptionally low-mounding spreading plant.
- Used for contrast and colour
- Carnation-like canary yellow flowers
- Small yellow leaves and pink flowers in July
- Can flower two times a year
- Very pretty planted with purple *Heuchera*

Vanderwolf Blue Pine

- The "perfect" pine
- Strong blue-green colour
- Natural habitat and shelter for birds
- Maintenance-free
- Symmetrical growth and ideal for small tree planting
- Specimen plant

Ice Blue Juniper

- Blue-green colour in summer
- Very low-growing
- Maintenance-free
- Excellent around basement windows
- Beautiful contrast plant
- Incredible growth over walls

Mr. Lincoln Rose

- 1965 Award Winner
- The best red rose . . . still to this day!
- Fragrant
- Produces lots of blooms
- Maintenance-free when planted with garlic and white geranium (perennial)
- Super for cut flowers and long lasting

Midnight Wine Weigela

- Exceptional purple leaf shrub
- Clusters of pink flowers in June
- Low-growing and maintenance-free
- Excellent low hedge
- Pest-free

Flowering Dogwood

- Specimen shrub tree
- Excellent for small backyards
- Lovely flowers in May and beautiful berries in summer
- Leaves show themselves in unusual format
- Farmers used to plant their corn according to when the dogwood flowered, which was the sign that frost was over.

Korean Spice

- Most fragrant!
- Clusters of fist-sized cream coloured flowers with pink centres
- Flowers for Mother's Day
- Attracts purple finches

Basil

- Leaves can be used in a tea. Very relaxing
- Rub basil leaves on insect bites, including bee stings
- Plant next to strawberries and tomatoes to improve taste

Monarda

- Attracts bees and hummingbirds (important pollinators)
- Extraordinary flowers: trumpet-like crimson filled with nectar
- Add tart tasting petals to salads made with Granny Smith apples
- Mix leaves with yogurt for a refreshing summer treat
- In the past, poultices of crushed monarda leaves were used to treat blemishes.
- This plant has three names: *Bergamot* for tea, *Beebalm* for bees and *Monarda* for beauty.
- Actually, Monarda gets its name from Nicolas Monardes, the 16th century Spanish physician and botanist.

Japanese Iris Palladia

- Does not spread like iris usually does—sorry!
- Beautiful gold or white variegated leaves
- Intense lilac-blue flowers in late May
- Leaves stay up all winter
- Pest- and disease-free
- Best planted in clumps

There are thousands of other plants you may want to recommend to your customer. Learn the characteristics and features of plants and upgrade constantly. This knowledge is your best asset in landscaping.

Remember that most revenue potential is in planting jobs. Nine out of ten companies lack expertise in plant knowledge and would benefit from upgrading or training and/or hiring staff with horticultural certification.

Most landscapers are "hardscape" specialists. I won most jobs because I was also a "plantsman." But I did not merely sell plants -- I sold colour, texture and fragrance!

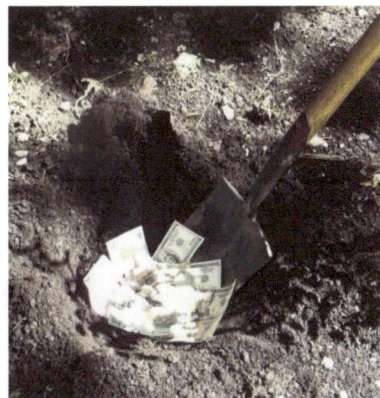

3.11 EFFECTIVE "CLOSERS"

You do not have unlimited time for a quotation. Look for ways you can skillfully bring the sales session to an end.

There are many ways to close a sale, but if you have done everything correctly up to this point, you may not have to formally close the sale because your customer has already made up his/her mind to work with you.

When it is time to close, you need to ask for the job. How you actually close depends on your personality. One good way to close is to ask indirectly.

Look at the examples on the next page.

EXAMPLES OF "CLOSERS"

- "I have marked your contract with anticipated start and finish dates. Do these meet with your approval?"
- May I make an appointment for you to come to the garden centre this Saturday so that we may select your plants?"[7]
- The best plants sell very early in the season. I need to have your commitment to get started with the selection process.
- I would like to start this job a week from Monday. If we cannot start Monday, unfortunately there will be a three-week delay.
- It takes about three weeks to obtain this colour of paving stones. May I place your order now?
- Have I satisfied all your concerns, including price?
- If you are unable to make a commitment regarding the date now, may I call you next week to confirm?

3.12 FOLLOW-UP AND FOLLOW-THROUGH

If the customer did not give you a definite answer at the "closer" stage, you may want to do a follow-up later. The follow-up means that you care enough about your business to send a thank you card for having had the opportunity to quote.

A follow-up phone call also lets your customers know that you are interested in the job and are willing to meet them again (and again and again, if necessary) to review the design, proposal and budgetary requirements.

If you have won the job, you deserve congratulations. But remember the "follow-through." A follow-through means getting the job done on time and on budget. You, your equipment and your employees are all integral components of the job.

---

[7] In my own landscaping company, I handled this differently. I would tell my customer that I would choose the best, most appropriate plants because I had access to and was able to purchase from multiple sources.

After the job is completed, visit the site to make sure that everything is as it should be. Send a pamphlet on maintenance procedures to your customers so that their investment is protected. Send a holiday card.

Keep your customers informed on developments of your company, for example, new techniques, new plants, etc. You can send them an annual newsletter or postcard. Since most landscape work is done through referrals, this type of marketing is very successful.

Keep your customers informed on developments

3.13 HOW MUCH WILL YOUR CUSTOMER SPEND?

This may be a sensitive issue for some customers. How do you tactfully guide your customers into revealing how much they are willing to spend for this job? The following questions and leading remarks may be helpful:

- A well-designed landscape today can cost about 10% of the value of a house.
- Do you want to use durable (i.e., lifetime) materials in your landscaping?
- Are you more interested in large (landscape size) shrubs and trees?
- It may cost (starting from) $25,000 to design and install your front entrance *if you want a long-lasting, pleasing and original concept*.
- The average landscape for a house in this neighbourhood is in the $25,000 range.

- Before we start with the design, this project will likely cost in the range of $$ to $$ but you should be aware that the project does not need to be completed in one season. That is, the job can be completed over a number of years.

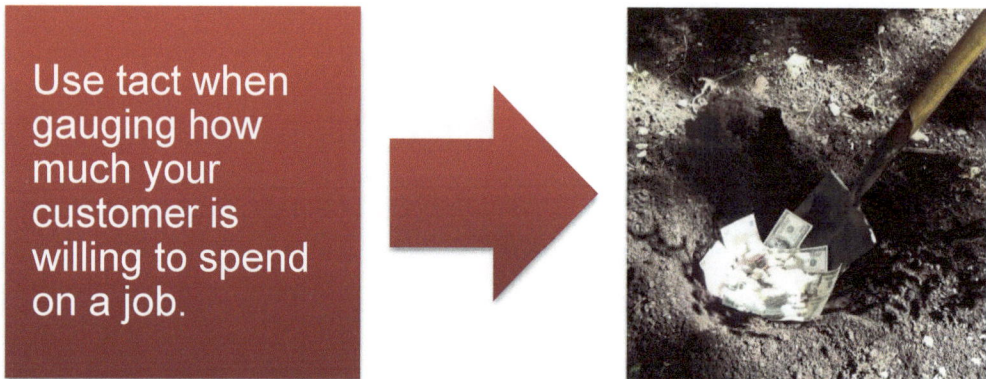

Use tact when gauging how much your customer is willing to spend on a job.

3.14 CUSTOMER CONCERNS

You have closed the sale. Now there are a few little details that must be clarified, and it is your job to reassure your customer of the following matters:

- Start date
- Finish date
- Job must be on budget, i.e., NO "extras."
- Job must be guaranteed — *totally*.
- Site must be cleaned up after completion of job.
- Neighbours must be notified.
- Customer must be completely satisfied before payment is made.
- Your company is fully insured.
- Customer will be given instructions on how to maintain landscape.
- Materials and plants are used as per quotation. For example, exact size, colour, etc.
- Site is inspected for a specified duration after completion of job.

CHAPTER 4

MASTER BUDGETING: THE FOUNDATION

This chapter includes sample master budgeting management forms for service companies. These forms are based on *What the Market will "Bare"* by J. Paul Lamarche.

Before calculating prices, you will need to create a budget. Note that the sample input forms shown for the overhead categories discussed in this chapter are print screens from the JPL System.

Samples of a budget report and annual overhead summary are shown on the next two pages, followed by data input forms.

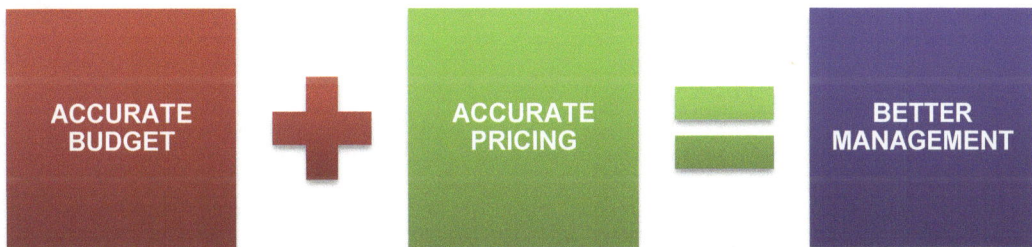

JPL System - Budgeting for Success 3000 1.05K

Annual Overhead Summary 2013

Overhead % : 22.87%

TOTAL FORECASTED NET SALES:	**$1,527,200.00**
TOTAL OVERHEAD:	**$349,378.00**

Administration	$66,240.00	4.34%
Advertising Media	$11,400.00	0.75%
Advertising Promotion	$15,000.00	0.98%
Bank Charges	$17,400.00	1.14%
Communication	$11,840.00	0.78%
Group Insurances	$18,000.00	1.18%
Insurances	$10,200.00	0.67%
Maintenance Building	$5,900.00	0.39%
Maintenance Property	$5,300.00	0.35%
Management	$69,000.00	4.52%
Office Supplies	$2,460.00	0.16%
Oil and Fuel	$12,000.00	0.79%
Professional Services	$15,050.00	0.99%
Rent/Mortage	$30,000.00	1.96%
Seminar & Training	$4,500.00	0.29%
Small Tools Purchases	$1,000.00	0.07%
Taxes & Licenses	$3,600.00	0.24%
Utilities	$4,150.00	0.27%
ROI - Office Equipment	$1,485.00	0.10%
ROI - Vehicle	$20,754.00	1.36%
ROI - Working Equipment	$5,849.00	0.38%
Maintn. - Office Equipment	$500.00	0.03%

ADMINISTRATION/RECEPTION

This category allows for compensation of bookkeeping, payroll, accounts payable/receivable, telephone answering and reception. Sometimes spouses of business owners perform these services without remuneration. This way, business owners are not responsible for employee benefits.

Many new companies make their first error here. They allow their spouse to handle reception and administration but do not pay them for their contribution to the company. It is important to charge your customers for these services. Enter a reasonable figure for these services — whether or not you are actually paying for them.

Many small or new companies "contract out" their administration/reception to other companies. Example: Hiring a bookkeeper at $15 to $20 per hour once a week to handle your accounting needs or hiring an answering service to take calls. When you contract out these services, there are no payroll taxes or state taxes.

JPL System - Budgeting for Success 3000 RC3 - Administrator

Salary calculation   2011

19. Dec. 2011

ID : A002   Position: Manager   Name: Bucet   First Name: Frank

Monthly Salary: $4,000.00   C.P.P.   E.I.   E.H.I.   W.S.I.B.   Vacation: Percent of salary in OH: 80.00%
4.40%   0.00%   0.00%   0.00%   0.00%   Net Salary: $3,340.80

To select click on the ID or Name field from the list below.

ID	Position	Name	First Name	OH%	Payment	C.P.P.	U.I.C.	E.H.I.	W.S.I.B.	Vacation	Net Salary
A001	Owner	Biber	John	100.00%	$5,500.00	4.40%	0.00%	0.00%	0.00%	0.00%	$5,742.00
A002	Manager	Bucet	Frank	80.00%	$4,000.00	4.40%	0.00%	0.00%	0.00%	0.00%	$3,340.80
B001	Administrator	Besancon	Anne	100.00%	$2,000.00	4.40%	2.60%	1.00%	4.65%	4.00%	$2,333.00
B002	Reception	Filou	Babette	100.00%	$1,600.00	4.40%	2.60%	1.00%	4.65%	4.00%	$1,866.40
D010	Yard operator	Schnyder	Tom	100.00%	$1,400.00	4.40%	2.60%	1.00%	4.65%	4.00%	$1,633.10

Department:	Payments :	Net Salary :	Per Year :
Administration	$3,600.00	$4,199.40	$50,392.80
Management	$9,500.00	$9,082.80	$108,993.60
Operating staff salary	$1,400.00	$1,633.10	$19,597.20

ADVERTISING/MEDIA

If you make an expensive corporate brochure and print enough for five years, you may wish to divide this cost over a number of years.

Example: A $10,000 brochure may be expensed as follows: $5,000 over two years or $2,000 over 5 years. Remember that this affects cash flow, in that you have paid in full for year 1 but may expense the cost over five years.

JPL System - Budgeting for Success 3000 RC3

Budget Year : 2011

19. Dec. 2011

Overhead-Category : Advertising Media

Change Category to: Advertising Media

| Category | Billboards | | | | | | Total Costs in 2011 | $13,500.00 |

April	$250.00	July	$250.00	October		January	
May	$250.00	August		November		February	
June	$250.00	September		December		March	$250.00

Delete the indicated Record !

Total Year : $1,250.00

Current Budget Year:

Category	Year	April	May	June	July	August	September	October	November	December	January
Billboards	$1,250.00	$250.00	$250.00	$250.00	$250.00						
Coupons	$750.00		$250.00	$250.00	$250.00						
Door Hangers	$2,500.00										
Newsletters	$2,500.00		$2,500.00								
Newspaper ads	$3,000.00	$500.00	$1,000.00	$1,000.00							
Post-Cards	$2,500.00			$2,500.00							
Television	$1,000.00	$1,000.00									

Record: 1 of 7   No Filter   Search

Select a previous year : 2010   Copy the selected year data to the current budget year.

Category	Year	April	May	June	July	August	September	October	November	December	January
Billboards	$1,250.00	$250.00	$250.00	$250.00	$250.00						
Coupons	$750.00		$250.00	$250.00	$250.00						
Door Hangers	$2,500.00										

Record: 1 of 7   No Filter   Search

ADVERTISING/PROMOTION

This is payment for company uniforms, signage, trade shows, company seminars, workshops, conventions, association dues, trades magazines, meals, gifts and entertainment. Note that many companies have a "50-50" agreement on uniforms with their employees. If you are paying only half, enter only your share on the appropriate line. Or, you may enter the full amount and add the employee contribution under Gross Sales as "Misc. Revenue."

- "Signage" is for vehicles, equipment, buildings and job sites.
- "Trade shows" includes labour and all related expenses.
- Signage can sometimes be a significant expense—perhaps over $10,000. In this case, it is better to spread the expense over two to five years so that it is not excessively high in one year.

JPL System - Budgeting for Success 3000 RC3			

Budget Year : 2011   19. Dec. 2011

Overhead-Category : Promotion

Change Category to: Promotion

Category	Gifts				Total Costs in 2011	$7,425.00
April	$100.00	July	$100.00	October	$100.00	January	$200.00
May	$100.00	August	$100.00	November	$100.00	February	$100.00
June	$100.00	September	$100.00	December	$300.00	March	$100.00

Delete the indicated Record !   Total Year : $1,500.00

Current Budget Year:

Category	Year	April	May	June	July	August	September	October	November	December	January
Chamber of Commerce	$500.00									$500.00	
Company uniform	$675.00										
Entertainment	$850.00									$850.00	
Gifts	$1,500.00	$100.00	$100.00	$100.00	$100.00	$100.00	$100.00	$100.00	$100.00	$300.00	$200.0
Landscape Ontario	$1,000.00						$1,000.00				
Meals	$1,500.00	$100.00	$100.00	$100.00	$100.00	$100.00	$100.00	$100.00	$100.00	$300.00	$200.0
Signage on vehicles	$1,000.00										
Trade shows	$400.00										$200.0

Record: 4 of 8   No Filter   Search

Select a previous year: 2010   Copy the selected year data to the current budget year.

Category	Year	April	May	June	July	August	September	October	November	December	January
Entertainment	$850.00									$850.00	
Gifts	$1,500.00	$100.00	$100.00	$100.00	$100.00	$100.00	$100.00	$100.00	$100.00	$300.00	$200.0
Landscape Ontario	$1,000.00						$1,000.00				

Record: 1 of 8   No Filter   Search

P R I C E , $ E L L ,   P R O D U C E   …   C A N   Y O U   D I G   I T ?

39

BAD DEBTS

Bad debts occur when customers do not pay for extras or as invoiced. Bad debts should never exceed 1% of total net sales. When customers do not pay for services, this becomes a cost of business. Someone has to pay for these costs, even though it is not the fault of your good customers. This is like experiencing a flat tire. No one is at fault, this is just a cost of doing business.

It is important to remember not to exceed 1% of net sales as a bad debt expense. If bad debt is higher than 1% of sales, overhead is increased and can become too high a burden. A high bad debt will have to be spread out over a number of years. EXAMPLE: A $10,000 bad debt may be spread over two years for a company that has $500,000 in sales. ($500,000 x 1% = $5,000). Expensing a high bad debt over one year would likely lead to an increase in overhead and have a negative effect on your competitiveness.

JPL System - Budgeting for Success 3000 RC3

Budget Year : 2011   19. Dec. 2011

Overhead-Category : Bad Debts

Change Category to: Bad Debts

Category: James (2006)   Total Costs in 2011 $14,400.00

Month	Amount	Month	Amount	Month	Amount	Month	Amount
April	$200.00	July	$200.00	October	$200.00	January	$200.00
May	$200.00	August	$200.00	November	$200.00	February	$200.00
June	$200.00	September	$200.00	December	$200.00	March	$200.00

Delete the indicated Record !

Total Year : $2,400.00

Current Budget Year:

Category	Year	April	May	June	July	August	September	October	November	December	January
James (2006)	$2,400.00	$200.00	$200.00	$200.00	$200.00	$200.00	$200.00	$200.00	$200.00	$200.00	$200.00
Smith (2007)	$12,000.00	$1,000.00	$1,000.00	$1,000.00	$1,000.00	$1,000.00	$1,000.00	$1,000.00	$1,000.00	$1,000.00	$1,000.00

Record: 1 of 2   No Filter   Search

Select a previous year : 2010   Copy the selected year data to the current budget year.

Category	Year	April	May	June	July	August	September	October	November	December	January
James (2006)	$2,400.00	$200.00	$200.00	$200.00	$200.00	$200.00	$200.00	$200.00	$200.00	$200.00	$200.00
Smith (2007)	$12,000.00	$1,000.00	$1,000.00	$1,000.00	$1,000.00	$1,000.00	$1,000.00	$1,000.00	$1,000.00	$1,000.00	$1,000.00

Record: 1 of 2   No Filter   Search

BANK CHARGES

This is for interest on lines of credit and operating loans, service charges on bank statements and cheques.[8] Note that interest on equipment and vehicles or building loans is entered in their respective categories, such as ROI on equipment, ROI on vehicles and rent.

EXAMPLE: If you borrow from the bank to purchase a $20,000 vehicle, total interest is added to principal and entered on your "ROI Vehicles" worksheet, so that you know the true cost of the vehicle. This also allows for "Return on Investment" on the real cost of the vehicle.

Current Budget Year:

Category	Year	April	May	June	July	August	September	October	November	December	January
Accounts receivable	$500.00		$250.00	$250.00							
Bonding	$200.00								$200.00		
Charge cards	$360.00									$360.00	
Interest on credit margin	$1,450.00	$400.00	$150.00							$100.00	$200.00
Service charges	$370.00	$25.00	$50.00	$50.00	$50.00	$50.00	$35.00	$35.00	$25.00	$20.00	

Select a previous year: 2010 — Copy the selected year data to the current budget year.

Category	Year	April	May	June	July	August	September	October	November	December	January
Account receivable	$500.00		$250.00	$250.00							
Bonding	$200.00								$200.00		
Charge cards	$360.00									$360.00	

---

[8] Another example would be fees on credit cards used by your customers to pay their bills. Note that about 75% of customers pay by credit card or debit card, and these fees can be quite high (anything over 1.75%). You may want to consider joining a group for a volume discount.

P R I C E , $ E L L ,   P R O D U C E   …   C A N   Y O U   D I G   I T ?

• • •

41

BANK PAYROLL

These are bank charges pertaining to payroll. Many companies (large and small) have their payroll handled by the bank. These charges are related to the number of employees you have each month.

FORECASTING INTEREST CHARGES

When preparing your books for income tax purposes, your accountant likely adds up all interest paid out and categorizes these costs under "interest expense." It is possible to predict your interest charges for your line of credit and/or your operating line, bank charges and short-term/long-term loans.

You can enter the interest charges once you have completed the 12-month fiscal budget. You can now determine your cash flow requirements based on total expenses and total revenues for each month. The balance at the end of each month will be cash flow and will give you a good idea on line of credit charges.

Always allow for the difference between what you pay monthly for a piece of equipment or vehicle vs. what the return on investment may show as a monthly or daily charge to your budget.

Of course, the longer the lifespan of this vehicle or equipment, the larger the difference between real monthly payments and ROI charges to your budget. This can turn into a cash shortfall.

EXAMPLE: You are paying $650 monthly for a vehicle loan, but because of *Return on Investment*, you may be showing a larger amount on your budget expense than what you actually pay out. Conversely, you may decide to pay off a loan for equipment/vehicles over two years, thereby creating a cash flow concern.

HOW MUCH CREDIT?

Look at your 12-Month Budget to see how much of a credit line you need each month. Look at the figure at the end of each month, after all costs of doing business are deducted from sales. Then enter the appropriate interest charges each month. Keep in mind that this must now be re-entered in your fiscal budget and recalculated.

The difficulty with this is estimating labour and material expense, as jobs can change from year to year. Your best bet is to look at your previous year's line of credit/interest expense and ask yourself if it will increase.

COMMUNICATION EXPENSE

This is for telephones, cellphones, mobile radios, beepers and answering services. Included are airtime, service charges and licenses. Internet, Key Tag[9], GPS and other service charges should be entered here.[10]

---

[9] Key Tag is a job monitoring system.

[10] I would not recommend taking out a contract when buying a cellphone. When you purchase a cellphone outright, even though initially it may cost more, you will have a better plan that costs less per month and is more flexible.

P R I C E , $ E L L , P R O D U C E … C A N Y O U D I G I T ?

• • •

44

EQUIPMENT: RETURN ON INVESTMENT (COMMUNICATION EQUIPMENT)

The ROI (Return on Investment) factor can be edited.[11]

NOTE RETURN ON INVESTMENT FORMULA

$$\frac{\text{Total cost of equipment (Total Price)}}{\text{(Lifespan in years)}} \times 1.5$$

You charge 1.5 times the cost per year for your communication equipment due to the fact that it will cost less to replace when you purchase new. Example: The cost of a cellphone in 1988 was $1,600, yet today a top-of-the-line model costs much less. It may even be free when included in a service contract. Therefore, if during the lifespan of your cellphone you collect 1.5 times the cost, you will have the cash to purchase new.

---

[11] You can set it to one or higher. I recommend that you do not set it higher than 2. Note that setting the factor to "1" is the same as setting it to "0".

P R I C E , $ E L L ,   P R O D U C E   …   C A N   Y O U   D I G   I T ?

• • •

45

EQUIPMENT: RETURN ON INVESTMENT

In this category, you are charging a monthly fee for each piece of equipment you own (paid off or on payments). To do this you need to identify the following: each piece of equipment, when you purchased it, how much you paid for it (interest charges included) and how long the equipment will last.[12] Note that you can also rent your equipment back to the business by checking the box "Renting Item?" and entering the number of days.

RETURN ON INVESTMENT FORMULA

$$\frac{\text{Total cost of equipment (Total Cost)}}{\text{(Lifespan in years)}} \times 2$$

---

[12]Use the JPL Fleet Cost Management System for easy calculation of ROI on equipment and vehicles. Available online at **www.jplbiz.ca**

GAS/OIL/FUEL

This includes gas, oil and fuel for vehicles and equipment, as well as for shop and yard equipment.[13]

JPL System - Budgeting for Success 3000 RC3

Budget Year : 2011 19. Dec. 2011

Overhead-Category : Oil and Fuel

Change Category to: Oil and Fuel

Category	Equipment Diesel				Total Costs in 2011	$47,000.00

April	$600.00	July	$600.00	October	$600.00	January	$600.00
May	$600.00	August	$600.00	November	$600.00	February	$600.00
June	$600.00	September	$600.00	December	$600.00	March	$600.00

Delete the indicated Record !   Total Year : $7,200.00

Current Budget Year:

Category	Year	April	May	June	July	August	September	October	November	December	January
Equipment Diesel	$7,200.00	$600.00	$600.00	$600.00	$600.00	$600.00	$600.00	$600.00	$600.00	$600.00	$600.00
Equipment gas	$9,800.00	$800.00	$800.00	$800.00	$800.00	$800.00	$800.00	$800.00	$800.00	$800.00	$1,000.00
Equipment oil	$2,400.00	$200.00	$200.00	$200.00	$200.00	$200.00	$200.00	$200.00	$200.00	$200.00	$200.00
Vehicle diesel	$10,800.00	$900.00	$900.00	$900.00	$900.00	$900.00	$900.00	$900.00	$900.00	$900.00	$900.00
Vehicle gas	$16,800.00	$1,400.00	$1,400.00	$1,400.00	$1,400.00	$1,400.00	$1,400.00	$1,400.00	$1,400.00	$1,400.00	$1,400.00

Record: 1 of 5   No Filter   Search

Select a previous year : 2010   Copy the selected year data to the current budget year.

Category	Year	April	May	June	July	August	September	October	November	December	January
Equipment Diesel	$7,200.00	$600.00	$600.00	$600.00	$600.00	$600.00	$600.00	$600.00	$600.00	$600.00	$600.0
Equipment gas	$9,800.00	$800.00	$800.00	$800.00	$800.00	$800.00	$800.00	$800.00	$800.00	$800.00	$1,000.0
Equipment oil	$2,400.00	$200.00	$200.00	$200.00	$200.00	$200.00	$200.00	$200.00	$200.00	$200.00	$200.0

Record: 1 of 5   No Filter   Search

---

[13] Some companies require an estimating system that incorporates *net cost per piece of equipment/vehicle* (including fuel, insurance and maintenance). This process is simplified with the JPL Fleet Cost Management System software. Order from: **www.jplbiz.ca**

GROUP INSURANCE

Medical, dental, life, hospital and travel insurance for company owners and/or managers (including employees).

Many employers continue to offer group insurance benefits to their employees, although laid off in winter months.[14] In some cases, companies ask these employees to contribute 50% to 75%. If you are using this option, you should include only the portion of the insurance costs that you are paying, or add the employees' contribution to "Miscellaneous Sales" under Revenue.

JPL System - Budgeting for Success 3000 RC3

Budget Year : **2011**   19. Dec. 2011

Overhead-Category : **Group Insurances**

Change Category to: Group Insurances

Category: Employee : 3x   Total Costs in 2011 $2,640.00

April	$120.00	July	$120.00	October	$120.00	January	$120.00
May	$120.00	August	$120.00	November	$120.00	February	$120.00
June	$120.00	September	$120.00	December	$120.00	March	$120.00

Delete the indicated Record !   Total Year : $1,440.00

Current Budget Year:

Category	Year	April	May	June	July	August	September	October	November	December	January
Employee : 3x	$1,440.00	$120.00	$120.00	$120.00	$120.00	$120.00	$120.00	$120.00	$120.00	$120.00	$120.00
Owner	$1,200.00	$100.00	$100.00	$100.00	$100.00	$100.00	$100.00	$100.00	$100.00	$100.00	$100.00

Record: 1 of 2   No Filter   Search

Select a previous year : 2010   Copy the selected year data to the current budget year.

Category	Year	April	May	June	July	August	September	October	November	December	January
Employee : 3x	$1,440.00	$120.00	$120.00	$120.00	$120.00	$120.00	$120.00	$120.00	$120.00	$120.00	$120.00
Owner	$1,200.00	$100.00	$100.00	$100.00	$100.00	$100.00	$100.00	$100.00	$100.00	$100.00	$100.00

Record: 1 of 2   No Filter   Search

---

[14] Employees may choose to leave their current employer to work at another company, if that company offers a health insurance perk.

INSURANCE

This category is for building, vehicle and equipment liability, professional and partnership insurance.[15]

JPL System - Budgeting for Success 3000 RC3

Budget Year :   **2011**   19. Dec. 2011

Overhead-Category : **Insurances**

Change Category to: Insurances

| Category | Building | | Total Costs in 2011 | $12,925.00 |

April		July		October		January	
May	$3,500.00	August		November		February	
June		September		December		March	

Delete the indicated Record !   Total Year : $3,500.00

Current Budget Year:

Category	Year	April	May	June	July	August	September	October	November	December	January
Building	$3,500.00		$3,500.00								
Equipment	$2,557.00			$2,557.00							
Liability	$795.00										
Partnership	$1,100.00										
Professional	$952.00										
Vehicle: 1999 Dumper/salt	$1,457.00										
Vehicle: 2000 3/4 ton	$782.00										
Vehicle: 2001 1 ton	$1,132.00										

Record: 1 of 9   No Filter   Search

Select a previous year : 2010   Copy the selected year data to the current budget year.

Category	Year	April	May	June	July	August	September	October	November	December	January
Building	$3,500.00		$3,500.00								
Equipment	$2,557.00			$2,557.00							
Liability	$795.00										

Record: 1 of 9   No Filter   Search

---

[15] I have an issue with the price disparity between insurance companies. I understand how a driver's age, accidents and tickets can affect insurance policies. It seems that the onus is on policyholders to obtain a variety of quotes and to educate themselves on how rates can be reduced.

P R I C E , $ E L L ,   P R O D U C E   …   C A N   Y O U   D I G   I T ?

49

MAINTENANCE (BUILDINGS)

All expenses to operate and maintain the building, such as repairs and improvements, cleaning supplies/services and coffee.

Budget Year : 2011

Overhead-Category : Maintenance Building

Change Category to: Maintenance Building

Category Disposal			
April	July $50.00	October $50.00	January
May $50.00	August $50.00	November $50.00	February
June $50.00	September $50.00	December $50.00	March

Total Costs in 2011 $2,850.00

Delete the indicated Record !

Total Year : $400.00

Current Budget Year:

Category	Year	April	May	June	July	August	September	October	November	December	January
Cleaning	$1,050.00	$100.00	$100.00	$100.00	$100.00	$100.00	$100.00	$100.00	$100.00	$100.00	$50.00
Disposal	$400.00		$50.00	$50.00	$50.00	$50.00	$50.00	$50.00	$50.00	$50.00	
Renovation and interest	$1,400.00									$1,000.00	$400.00

Record: 2 of 3   No Filter   Search

Select a previous year : 2010   Copy the selected year data to the current budget year.

Category	Year	April	May	June	July	August	September	October	November	December	January
Cleaning	$1,050.00	$100.00	$100.00	$100.00	$100.00	$100.00	$100.00	$100.00	$100.00	$100.00	$50.0
Disposal	$400.00		$50.00	$50.00	$50.00	$50.00	$50.00	$50.00	$50.00	$50.00	
Renovation and interest	$1,400.00									$1,000.00	$400.0

Record: 1 of 3   No Filter   Search

A NOTE ON RENOVATIONS

Under the renovation category, all forecasted expenses for the fiscal year are shown. The $1,400 expense is not a large amount for renovations; however, if the amount is more than 2% of sales, I suggest that you make a new expense category in your fiscal budget. Call this LEASEHOLD IMPROVEMENTS and divide the amount by an appropriate number of years, thereby limiting the burden on your overhead, so that you remain competitive. Include all employee hours that pertain to renovations. Remember that you will probably pay in full for the renovations, so take this into account for your cash flow needs.

MAINTENANCE (PROPERTY)

This refers to maintenance costs such as grass cutting, flower planting, signs, snow removal and site improvements. Remember that if your employees are doing any of this work at your premises, you need to enter the wages you pay them plus payroll taxes.

Often companies conclude that it is less expensive to subcontract this type of work. However, many businesses continue to use their own employees in an effort to keep their best employees occupied, even when this costs more.

JPL System - Budgeting for Success 3000 RC3

Budget Year : 2011　　19. Dec. 2011

Overhead-Category : Maintenance Property

Change Category to: Maintenance Property

Category: Grass cutting

Total Costs in 2011　$1,750.00

April	July $100.00	October $100.00	January
May $100.00	August $100.00	November	February
June $100.00	September $100.00	December	March

Delete the indicated Record !

Total Year : $600.00

Current Budget Year:

Category	Year	April	May	June	July	August	September	October	November	December	January
Flowers	$250.00		$125.00						$125.00		
Grass cutting	$600.00		$100.00	$100.00	$100.00	$100.00	$100.00	$100.00			
Landscaping	$500.00	$500.00									
Snow removal	$400.00									$100.00	$100.00

Record: 2 of 4　No Filter　Search

Select a previous year : 2010　　Copy the selected year data to the current budget year.

Category	Year	April	May	June	July	August	September	October	November	December	January
Flowers	$250.00		$125.00						$125.00		
Grass cutting	$600.00		$100.00	$100.00	$100.00	$100.00	$100.00	$100.00			
Landscaping	$500.00	$500.00									

Record: 1 of 4　No Filter　Search

MAINTENANCE (EQUIPMENT)

All expenses to keep equipment in top shape, such as overhauls, tune-ups, paint jobs and parts replacement are entered under maintenance. If you engage your employees to do any of the above maintenance work, you need to enter the amount paid to them, plus applicable payroll taxes.[16]

CAPITALIZING SOME REPAIRS

For income tax purposes, your accountant may capitalize some repairs, especially larger ones. A large repair, i.e., an engine at $15,000 or more, is best expensed over a number of years to reduce the impact on overhead. Remember potential cash flow shortfalls in this case. [17]

MAINTENANCE (VEHICLES)

Same as equipment and includes all costs for vehicles used in business including company cars. If you engage your employees to do any of the above maintenance work, you need to enter the amount paid to them, plus applicable payroll taxes. A large repair, i.e., an engine at $15,000 or more is best expensed over a number of years to reduce the impact on overhead. Remember potential cash flow shortfall in this case.

EXAMPLE

If you pay $15,000 for a motor in the current fiscal year, it is advisable to enter only $5,000 in this year's budget and $5,000 in each of the next two budgets – *if you foresee a three-year lifespan for the motor and vehicle.*

---

[16] Unless you have an employee (for example a mechanic) whose wages (part-time or full-time) are entered under overhead.

[17] For example, if you pay $15,000 for a motor in the current fiscal year, it is advisable to enter only $5,000 in this year's budget and $5,000 in each of the next two budgets – *if you foresee a three-year lifespan for the motor and vehicle.*

Remember that at the end of the fiscal year, your profit will be $10,000 short because you paid for the engine in the current fiscal year.

JPL System - Budgeting for Success 3000 RC3

Edit   2011   Operating Costs

Pickup 1ton   DFRT-5845

19. Dec. 2011

Type of Cost : Tune-up   New Operating Cost Record :

April	$180.00	July	$120.00	October	$120.00	January	$120.00
May		August		November		February	
June		September		December		March	

Delete this Record

Current Year: 2011

Type OP Costs	April	May	June	July	August	September	October	November	December	January	February	March
Tires	$1,280.00											$1,680.00
PWR train								$2,650.00				
Tune-up	$180.00			$120.00			$120.00			$120.00		
Misc									$1,200.00			

Select a previous year : 2010

Type OP Costs	April	May	June	July	August	September	October	November	December	January	February	March
Tune-up											$685.00	

MANAGEMENT

Wages, salaries or draws for the owners and/or managers who do not work on the job site or are not charged to the job on an hourly basis are included here. Some owners/managers spend 50% of their time[18] actively working on the job site and should split their incomes by categorizing 50% of their pay under "Cost of Goods Sold" and the remaining 50% under "Management." Note that small business owners who earn all their wages actively working on the job should enter a smaller amount under "Management." This, in effect, charges the customer for sales, design and management time.[19] A pension plan is the only payroll tax for owners, unless the company is incorporated, in which case full payroll taxes apply. Owners may now be eligible for Employment Insurance.

---

[18] Some managers may spend more than 50% of their time on the front line; others spend less time.
[19] This way the owner is compensated for all his/her time.

PERSONNEL COSTS (SALARY CALCULATION)

These costs directly affect the overhead of your company.[20]

JPL System - Budgeting for Success 3000 RC3 - Administrator

Salary calculation   2011

19. Dec. 2011

ID: A002   Position: Manager   Name: Bucet   First Name: Frank

Monthly Salary: $4,000.00   C.P.P.   E.I.   E.H.I.   W.S.I.B.   Vacation: Percent of salary in OH: 80.00%
                            4.40%   0.00% 0.00%   0.00%   0.00%   Net Salary: $3,340.80

To select click on the ID or Name field from the list below.

ID	Position	Name	First Name	OH%	Payment	C.P.P.	U.I.C.	E.H.I.	W.S.I.B.	Vacation	Net Salary
A001	Owner	Biber	John	100.00%	$5,500.00	4.40%	0.00%	0.00%	0.00%	0.00%	$5,742.00
A002	Manager	Bucet	Frank	80.00%	$4,000.00	4.40%	0.00%	0.00%	0.00%	0.00%	$3,340.80
B001	Administrator	Besancon	Anne	100.00%	$2,000.00	4.40%	2.60%	1.00%	4.65%	4.00%	$2,333.00
B002	Reception	Filou	Babette	100.00%	$1,600.00	4.40%	2.60%	1.00%	4.65%	4.00%	$1,866.40
D010	Yard operator	Schnyder	Tom	100.00%	$1,400.00	4.40%	2.60%	1.00%	4.65%	4.00%	$1,633.10

Department:	Payments :	Net Salary :	Per Year :
Administration	$3,600.00	$4,199.40	$50,392.80
Management	$9,500.00	$9,082.80	$108,993.60
Operating staff salary	$1,400.00	$1,633.10	$19,597.20

productive employees = reduction in overhead

---

[20] JPL Budgeting and Estimating 3000 allows you to allocate the percentage of time each employee spends in overhead and then allocates that percentage to overhead. Our system is simple and accurate.

PERSONNEL COSTS (HOURLY)

These costs are not part of overhead. They are part of "Costs of Goods Sold" and are required for calculating your estimate and for "by the hour" jobs.[21] Note that downtime can easily be allocated separately for each employee.

Examples would include:

- Sales
- Cashiers
- Loaders
- Landscaping
- Tree planting
- Container planting
- Delivery services
- Design services

---

[21] "Rate for hourly charge sales" is shown as many independent garden centres (IGCs) do deliveries, plant trees, install landscapes or provide consultation to their customers.

OFFICE SUPPLIES

This is for stamps, photocopying, envelopes, letterhead, business forms, business cards, invoices, pens, pencils, miscellaneous office items, computer forms and software, as well as materials needed for sales presentations by your sales/design staff.

JPL System - Budgeting for Success 3000 RC3

Budget Year : 2011   19. Dec. 2011

Overhead-Category : Office Supplies

Change Category to: Office Supplies

| Category | Toner | | | | | Total Costs in 2011 | $1,845.00 |

April	$180.00	July	$180.00	October	$180.00	January	$180.00
May		August		November		February	
June		September		December		March	

Delete the indicated Record !   Total Year : $720.00

Current Budget Year:

Category	Year	April	May	June	July	August	September	October	November	December	January
Envelopes	$95.00	$15.00			$15.00			$15.00		$50.00	
Ink	$274.00	$89.00				$90.00				$95.00	
Paper ink printer	$216.00	$18.00	$18.00	$18.00	$18.00	$18.00	$18.00	$18.00	$18.00	$18.00	$18.00
Paper laser printer	$540.00	$90.00		$90.00		$90.00		$90.00		$120.00	$60.00
Toner	$720.00	$180.00			$180.00			$180.00			$180.00

Record: 5 of 5   No Filter   Search

Select a previous year : 2010   Copy the selected year data to the current budget year.

Category	Year	April	May	June	July	August	September	October	November	December	January
Misc	$2,775.00	$500.00	$175.00	$175.00	$175.00	$175.00	$175.00	$175.00	$175.00	$450.00	$200.00

Record: 1 of 1   No Filter   Search

OFFICE EQUIPMENT: RETURN ON INVESTMENT (ROI)

This is the amount charged to the budget for all equipment in order to earn "Return on Investment."

EXAMPLE OF RETURN ON INVESTMENT ON OFFICE EQUIPMENT

A $4,800 photocopier with a lifespan of 4 years equals a cost of $1,200 per year. However, in this case, in order to calculate ROI (Return on Investment) we multiply by 1.5 instead of by 2, because the next photocopier (and most office equipment) will cost less to replace.

A large repair is best expensed over a number of years to reduce the impact on overhead. Remember that there may be a potential cash flow shortfall in this case. Do not forget to include the residual value of your office equipment, as this lowers the net cost of the equipment. In the above ROI Office/Communication Equipment input form, residual value has been set to $0.00.

PROFESSIONAL SERVICES

This is for lawyers, accountants, consultants, credit collection or any other type of service from a professional that you would require during the course of operating your business.[22]

---

[22] I would recommend that you use the same software as your accountant to do your company bookkeeping. This can save you hundreds of dollars each year.

P R I C E , $ E L L ,   P R O D U C E   ...   C A N   Y O U   D I G   I T ?

• • •

59

RENT/MORTGAGE

Rent/Mortgage refers to payment for rental of building/land or the amount you enter in the budget for use of your land and house. Rent or mortgage should never exceed 3% of sales. If you use one room in a four room house, you may legally deduct 25% of all expenses, including mortgage interest.[23] Even if you do not actually write a cheque for the rent of your home and/or land for business use, you must enter a reasonable amount in your budget. Otherwise, you are offering your home and land free of charge and are thereby distorting the budget, resulting in a lower overhead cost, which in turn distorts the break-even point.

---

[23] This is calculated in square footage. Your total office square footage should equal 25% of the total square footage of the house.

SMALL TOOLS PURCHASES

This is for all small tools under $500 in value. Each year, you replace many of your tools; therefore, enter full value of these tools into the budget. Your "Small Tools Purchases" should not exceed 0.5% of sales. Anything above this amount is likely evidence of theft or negligence.[24]

Current Budget Year:

Category	Year	April	May	June	July	August	September	October	November	December	January
Gloves	$500.00	$120.00			$120.00			$260.00			
Safety equipment	$680.00		$680.00								
Small power tool	$0.00										
Wheel barrow	$180.00	$180.00									

Select a previous year : 2010

Category	Year	April	May	June	July	August	September	October	November	December	January
Summaries	$950.00		$300.00	$50.00			$250.00				

---

[24] Many businesses now expect employees to purchase their own safety wear, as well as hand tools and gloves.

P R I C E , $ E L L ,   P R O D U C E   ...   C A N   Y O U   D I G   I T ?

• • •

61

TAXES/LICENCES

This is for business and property taxes, vehicle licences and registration.

P R I C E , $ E L L ,   P R O D U C E   …   C A N   Y O U   D I G   I T ?

62

UTILITIES

This is for hydro/gas/water/fuel: 100% for companies with corporate buildings and offices and up to 25% for offices run from your home.

P R I C E , $ E L L ,   P R O D U C E   …   C A N   Y O U   D I G   I T ?

• • •

63

VEHICLE PURCHASES/RETURN ON INVESTMENT (ROI)[25]

This is for small trucks and cars. Even if the vehicle is paid off, you should continue to enter the same amount per month during the lifespan of the vehicle. This allows for funds to purchase the next vehicle.[26]

Note that the checked box indicates that the vehicle is rented to the company and is expected to be used 225 days of the year.

---

[26] The JPL Fleet Cost Management System makes this work easy and accurate. Order your copy at **www.jplbiz.ca**

RETURN ON INVESTMENT FORMULA[27]

$$\frac{\text{Total cost of Vehicle (Net Price)}}{\text{(Lifespan in years)}} \times 2 = \text{Total cost per year}$$

EXAMPLE:

RETURN ON INVESTMENT FOR A $40,000 VEHICLE

(Includes Taxes and Financing Charges,
Less Residual — Resale Value After 8 Years)

1. Divide the $40,000 by the expected lifespan of the vehicle (8 years)
2. This is equal to $5,000 per year.
3. Multiply that amount by 2 to get "Return on Investment."
4. Return on investment is therefore $10,000 per year over the vehicle's lifespan of 8 years, which equals $80,000.

*This equals $40,000 for the initial cost of the vehicle and $40,000 to purchase a replacement.

---

[27] Use this formula if you intend to bury your equipment and vehicles in overhead.

The JPL Fleet Cost Management System allows you to take your equipment and vehicles out of overhead and rent them back to your company and your customers. This facilitates tracking and allows you to manage your equipment and management costs more accurately.

FISCAL BUDGET 200-

	LANDSCAPING	MAINTENANCE	SNOW REMOVAL	COMMENTS
FORECASTED SALES (NOT GST)				
Contract sales				
Hourly charge sales				
Equipment charge sales				
Material sales				
GROSS SALES				
Less: subcontracting				Amount paid for subcontracting
Less: Returns/Allowances				Cost of labour and materials to fix or replace deficiencies
NET SALES				
Cost of goods sold (C.G.S.)				
Materials				Price you pay for materials including tax (Prov. Or state)
Disposal				Payment for dumping or composting
Equipment Rentals outsource				Equip. rentals from outside companies for completing job
Equipment Rentals in-house				
Vehicle Rentals outsource				
Vehicle Rentals in-house				
Total Purchases C.G.S.				
LABOUR				
Owner / Operator wages				Percentage on job
Supervisor wages				Supervisor/foreperson on job or in store
Employee wages				All employee hours charged to you
Employee Benefits/Payroll tax				% of labour expense
WSIB				Employee work insurance
TOTAL LABOUR				25% for landscape, 42% for maintenance
TOTAL COST OF GOODS SOLD				
GROSS PROFIT				
OVERHEAD				
Administration / Reception				Payroll/Accounts Payable/Telephone Reception
Management (MG)				Manager/Owner (Wages or Salary for work off job site
Professional services				Accountant fees for taxation/accounting/consulting
Communication expense				Cellular phone and charges/mobile radio/beepers
Insurance				Vehicles/building/liability
Group insurance				Medical/dental for employees and owners
Bad debts				Should not be more than 1 to 1.5%
Bank charges				Service charges for cheques/lines of credit/operating loans
Rent / mortgage				Office/garage/ (fee charged to budget to obtain ROI)
Taxes / licenses				
Advertising / promotion				Uniforms/events/entertainment/associations/magazines
Advertising / media				Catalogue/media/magazines/newsletters/flyers
Sales expense				Designers/sales staff
Seminars / Training				Staff training
Maintenance: building				Repairs to buildings
Maintenance: property				Repairs to property
Maintenance: equipment				Repairs to equipment/tools
Maintenance: vehicles				Repairs to vehicles
ROI Office equipment				Charges to budget for existing equipment, including ROI
ROI Communication equipment				Charges to budget for existing equipment, including ROI
ROI Equipment				Charges to budget for existing equipment, including ROI
ROI Shop equipment				Charges to budget for existing equipment, including ROI
ROI Vehicles				Charges to budget for existing equipment, including ROI
Fuel & Oil				For vehicles/equipment
Utilities				Hydro/gas/fuel/water
Office supplies				Stamps/invoices/letterhead/miscellaneous
Small tool purchases				Small tools/blades/chains, etc.
TOTAL OVERHEAD				32% of total sales-benchmark figure for landscape company
				42% of total sales-benchmark figure for maintenance company
TOTAL EXPENSE				Cost of Goods Sold and Overhead Expense
PROFIT/LOSS				

P R I C E , $ E L L ,   P R O D U C E   …   C A N   Y O U   D I G   I T ?

66

ARE YOU INCLUDING RETURN ON INVESTMENT IN YOUR BUDGET?

When you budget for your operating costs, you should also be accounting for "return on investment" (ROI) on all equipment and vehicles. Think of return on investment (ROI) as interest. If you don't make interest, the value of your assets depreciates. If you want to charge for vehicles and equipment on a per day basis, you need to know the full cost, lifespan and residual value of your vehicles and equipment. The reasoning behind charging your customers adequately for every vehicle on every job is to enable you to recoup every penny you paid over a vehicle's lifespan and allow for a return on your investment. If you are using a "minimum daily rate" system in your company, you should also have a system in place for calculating ROI. This is essential for all equipment and vehicles because the minimum daily rate pays both for the purchase and the return on investment. What is your maintenance cost per vehicle? What is your rent-out charge per day? **JPL Fleet Cost Management System** has the answers.

- ✓ Integrate vehicle and equipment costs with operating costs
- ✓ Calculate an accurate minimum daily rate that pays both for the purchase and ROI, enabling you to have the funds available when the time comes to replace vehicles and equipment.
- ✓ Reduce financing charges, thereby reducing overhead.
- ✓ Obtain your true overhead figures so that you can create an accurate per day price for estimating purposes.

This powerful user-friendly software tracks all applicable operating costs (maintenance, insurance, taxes, etc.) to calculate the true cost of all types of vehicles and equipment. The JPL Fleet Cost Management System is customizable to suit fleet requirements for companies of all sizes and types.

JPL SYSTEMS HELP YOU TO MAKE BETTER DECISIONS IN TODAY'S VERY COMPETITIVE BUSINESS CLIMATE.

CHAPTER 5

ALL YOU NEED IS A CALCULATOR? ARE YOU SERIOUS?

5.1 WHAT CAN I CHARGE FOR MY SERVICES?

Years of hands-on experience have shown me there are some jobs not worth doing if I want to make money. Through the creation of a proven pricing system, I now bid confidently and competitively. While it requires consistent record keeping, my system is simple and will show you what you need to charge to be profitable[28].

"What can I charge for my services?" is the number one question among entrepreneurs. Some entrepreneurs believe that estimating is pricing according to what the market will bear. For others, it may be a matter of pulling out the Yellow Pages, calling half a dozen competitors, averaging out their (unit) prices and using that as a price.

Many industries simply take a markup percentage on top of their goods or material costs. This can work well for retailers but is not good for service industries like landscape contractors. Service contractors may know the exact amount of material and labour hours required to do a job; however, many do not understand how to price so that overhead, ROI and profit are included.

No two companies will have the same overhead. A proper strategy for pricing requires that you find your cost of doing business, so you can establish your break-even point per person hour, per service and per job.

---

[28] A well-done landscaping job adds investment value to your customer's home. Shouldn't you be rewarded for your efforts? Your profit is your reward.

Find your cost of doing business

to establish your break-even point

My step-by-step plan allows you to go beyond break-even points or price for profits, and allows you to determine which jobs to bid on and how to use equipment profitably.

5.2 ESSENTIAL FIRST STEP: DETERMINE OVERHEADS

I cannot stress enough that you must have an accurate picture of your true overhead costs. Sure, it means some discipline, but it will give you confidence in your bidding and long-term success. Determining the costs of doing business requires the commitment to maintain a 12-month budget.

In fact, nine out of ten service companies don't do any budgeting at all. Some don't even reconcile their bank statements at the end of the month. For others, records are kept in their heads or their pockets. I know one individual who kept revenues in one pocket and expenses in the other[29].

---

[29] He is still doing this today, because it works for him.

PRICE, $ELL, PRODUCE ... CAN YOU DIG IT?

• • •

69

Overhead represents all your costs that cannot be allocated to specific jobs. Be sure to include your own salary[30]. Don't forget to include the salary of your spouse. If you actually work on the job and are charged hourly to the job, then you only need to enter an incremental amount under salary (30% to 50% of net sales) to cover your time for estimating, selling, designing, etc. Use your accounting software.

Once you get set up, you can calculate the cost of your overhead more accurately. Note that accounting software enters only cash or cheques paid out for invoices. One of the most important items in your overhead is ROI or return on investment.

After your equipment is paid off, you should continue to charge your overhead the monthly fee you were paying on your equipment. This allows you to collect the funds to pay cash for your next piece of equipment. It takes a little patience, but the results are worth the effort.

5.3 NEXT: FORECAST YOUR SALES

Now you must forecast a number to represent your forecasted net sales. This means sales, less sales taxes and subcontractor costs. In determining this figure, be absolutely realistic about using a number pegged as closely to your real sales as possible. DO NOT use this as an opportunity to set yourself an unrealistic sales goal. The system gives you plenty of chances to boost your profit margins later on.

---

[30] A good salary is a healthy salary. It should not be more than 10% of net sales and never less than what you pay your best employee.

| GROSS SALES | − | Sales tax + sub-contractor costs | = | forecasted net sales |

5.4 KNOW YOUR OVERHEAD PERCENTAGE

Now you have two important numbers: your annual overhead cost and your annual sales forecast number. Divide your overhead cost in dollars by your forecasted net sales in dollars to get a percentage figure: your overhead expense as a percentage of forecasted net sales, or simply "overhead percentage."

Knowing this percentage is essential to using the JPL system. Knowing your overhead percentage also essential for gaining financial control of your company.[31].

5.5 DO THE MATH: OVERHEAD PERCENTAGE

A sample overhead expense of $175,000 divided by forecasted net sales of $450,000 results in a 39% overhead percentage. Knowing this percentage allows you to calculate your break-even point on any job down the road. In other words, the lowest amount you can charge for a job before you start losing money.

Typical overhead percentages range from 40-50% for smaller horticultural entrepreneurs and can go down to 17% for the largest companies. This should help you to realize why small companies are at a disadvantage in the tendering process.

---

[31] This would apply to any system.

5.6 GET YOUR MAGIC NUMBER

Once you know your overhead percentage, the JPL Estimating System prompts you to enter your overhead percentage and create a "Magic Number" for estimating purposes. Let's say your overhead percentage is 39%.

To arrive at your "Magic Number," subtract your overhead figure from 100%, (100% - 39%).

In this case it would be 61%.

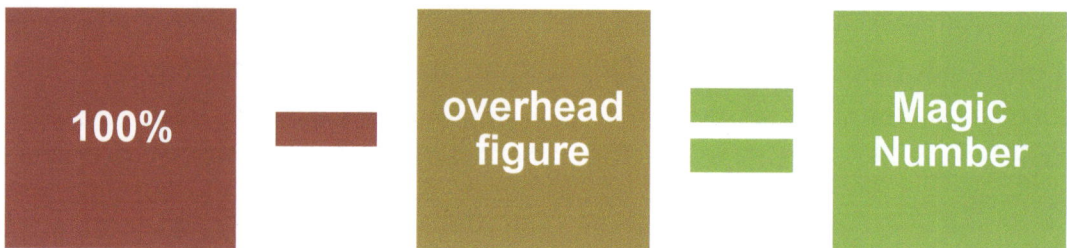

100% − overhead figure = Magic Number

5.7 USING YOUR MAGIC NUMBER

To use the Magic Number to quote jobs, start by adding up your direct job costs, called Cost of Goods Sold, for a specific job. In broad terms, these costs will include materials, disposal, labour, equipment rentals (all at exact cost to you less sales taxes).

COSTS OF GOODS SOLD INCLUDE

equipment rentals

materials

labour

disposal

Now you have all the information you need to complete the job.

Note that determining accurate labour costs is a little tricky. The benefits you pay are significant and are properly allocated here, rather than in your overhead.

In the horticulture industry, benefits typically cost another 15% to 20% above base wages. You should also factor in downtime, if you are charging your customers by the hour rather than a quoted price.

If you work alongside your crew on a job site, build in an hourly rate for yourself on top of your salary, which is part of overhead.

Take the dollar figure for your direct job costs and divide by your Magic Number to arrive at your break-even price for the job.

If you work on the job site 50% of the time, or 2000 hours per year this works out to 1000 hours on the job site.

If your goal is to earn $50,000 per year, then you will need $25 per hour to attain this.

5.8 DO THE MATH: A SAMPLE QUOTE

- You have calculated that the direct costs on a job will be $1710.
- Your Magic Number is 61%.
- Divide $1,710 by 61% on your calculator.
- Your break-even price for the job is $2,803.28.

We have been using 61% as the Magic Number. Stated a different way, it means that your jobs must be quoted so 39% of your earnings go to cover your overhead. If you wish to make 15% profit on this job, then you take your break-even cost of $2,803.28 to do the job and divide it by 85%.

(100% - your desired profit of 15% = 85%)

The quoted price comes in at $3,297.97. Note that if you multiplied your break-even cost to do the job by 15%, you would arrive at $3,223.77.[32]

As an experienced professional, you can jot down a few numbers and get a pretty good idea of your direct costs when you do a take-off. You can pull out a calculator, punch in your cost and simply divide by your Magic Number to quote the job. The customer will have no idea what you just did, but you are

---

[32] While this is not a big difference, you are invited to mail the difference to me, if it means so little to you!

confident all your costs, both overhead and direct, are covered, as well as your profit margin. If a customer offers you X dollars to do a job, you can quickly calculate your break-even point and stand your ground.

Direct Costs ÷ **Magic Number** = **Break-even Cost for Job**

CHAPTER 6

CHARGING FOR YOUR SERVICES:
YOUR VALUE, YOUR NAME AND YOUR REPUTATION

6.1 OVERHEAD AND PRICING (A REVIEW)

Remember that no two companies will have the same overhead. A proper strategy for pricing requires that you find your cost of doing business so you can establish your break-even point per person hour, per service and per job.

Our step-by-step plan allows you to go beyond break-even points and price for profits. You will learn how to determine which jobs to bid on, and how to use equipment profitably.

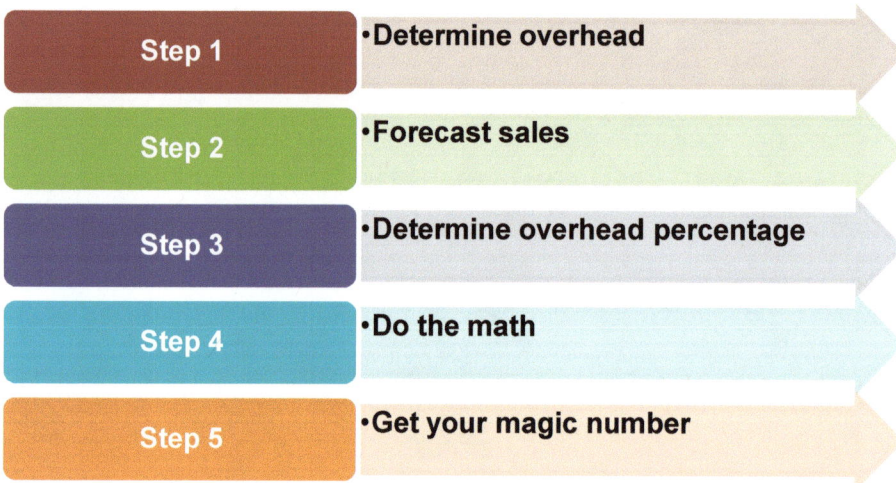

Step 1	•Determine overhead
Step 2	•Forecast sales
Step 3	•Determine overhead percentage
Step 4	•Do the math
Step 5	•Get your magic number

Knowing your overhead percentage allows you to calculate your break-even point on any job down the road.

The break-even point is actually the lowest amount you should charge for a job before you start losing money. Now, because you know your break-even costs, customers will not be able to talk you down in price.[33]

(FIG. 6.1) OVERHEAD PERCENTAGE EXAMPLE

OVERHEAD EXPENSE	FORCASTED NET SALES	OVERHEAD PERCENTAGE
$175,000	$450,000	39%

Calculate as follows to obtain the overhead percentage:

$197,500 ÷ forecasted net sales of $450,000
= 39% overhead percentage.
= $1,129 overhead per day, based on 5 days per week for 35 working weeks.

Typical overhead percentages range from 40 to 50% for smaller horticultural entrepreneurs, and can go down to 17% or less for the largest companies. This demonstrates clearly why small companies are at a disadvantage in the tendering process.[34]

Calculate as follows:

(100% - 39%)
= 61%

---

[33] Unless you are willing to lose money!

[34] They should avoid bidding on such jobs, until their company is larger and the corresponding overhead is lower.

6.2 REAL LIFE ESTIMATING

To use the *Magic Number* to quote jobs, start by adding up your direct job costs[35] for a specific job. In broad terms, these costs will include materials, disposal, labour, equipment rentals and anything else you need to complete the job.[36]

Note that determining accurate labour costs is a little tricky. The benefits you pay are significant and are properly allocated here rather than in your overhead. In the horticulture industry, employee payroll costs typically add another 20% to base wages.

You should also factor in downtime, if you are charging your customers by the hour rather than a quoted price. In addition, if you work alongside your crew on a job site, you should build in an hourly rate for yourself on top of your salary, which is part of overhead. Note that subcontractors are not and never should be part of Cost of Goods Sold.

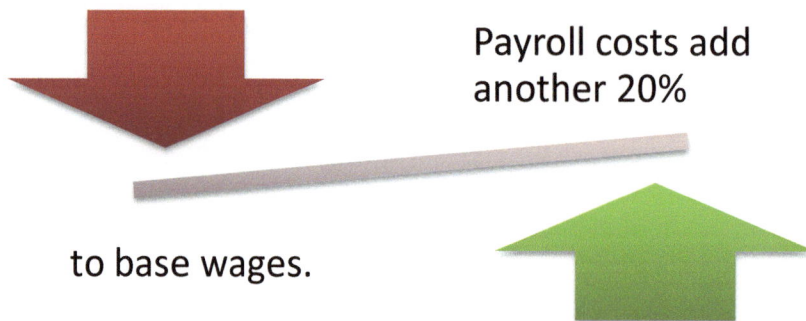

Payroll costs add another 20% to base wages.

Take the dollar figure for your direct job costs, and divide by your *Magic Number* to arrive at your break-even price for the job.

---

[35] Direct job costs are also called *cost of goods sold*.
[36] (All exact costs to you minus sales taxes).

6.3 SAMPLE QUOTATION (A REVIEW)

Here are the important figures:

- The direct job costs are $1,710.
- Your *Magic Number* is 61%. This means that your jobs must be quoted so 39% of your earnings go to cover your overhead.
- Divide $1,710 by 61 % on your calculator to get your break-even price for the job: $2,803.28.
- If you wish to make 15% profit on this job, then you take your break-even cost of $2,803.28 to do the job and divide it by 85%. Calculate as follows:

(100 – your desired profit of 15% = 85%)

The quoted price then comes in at $3,297.98. Note that if you multiplied your break-even cost by 15%, you would arrive at $3,223.77.[37]

6.4 BEYOND THE FORMULA

Your profit margin is what your whole business is about, and you set those goalposts. For contracting, 10% is a good target, and most well-managed companies achieve or exceed this margin.

There will be times, however, when you might want to "buy" a job. In other words, bid at break-even or less for one reason or another. The system allows you to do just that, by omitting the desired profit from your formula. The result is a bid that reflects a true break-even cost and shows you exactly how much money you are willing to use.

---

[37] While this is not a big difference, you are invited to mail the difference to me, if it means so little to you!

You achieve your objective, while you have all of your costs covered, unlike many other contractors who work harder and harder to go backwards at a faster rate.

Once you meet your targeted net sales figure for the fiscal year, all additional net sales come with only a fraction of overhead, as you have covered your forecasted overhead for the year.

The JPL Estimating System is simple. Just complete the information to make the formula work for you. However, keep in mind that the accounting adage "garbage in = garbage out" applies here, too. If you enter the wrong amount for labour, or miss the mark on cost of materials, then you will not arrive at the right price for your service.

If you follow the steps outlined in this chapter, the JPL Estimating System can easily be incorporated into your estimating strategy.[38]

---

[38] The JPL Estimating System can be fine-tuned for more accuracy with factors such as labour costs, depreciation and return on investment.

6.5 USING THE RIGHT ESTIMATING SYSTEM

Are you using the right estimating system? Take the quiz in the next section.

ESTIMATING QUIZ

This quiz is for service contractors. Take this quiz to find out if you are using the right pricing or estimating system. The answers can be found following the quiz.

1. You want a 25% profit on $10,000. What is 25% profit on $10,000?

   a) $2,500
   b) $3,000
   c) $3,333.33
   d) $_____?

2. A benchmark service contracting company with sales of $450,000 should have an ideal overhead[39] (as a percentage of sales) of:

   a) 20%
   b) 30%
   c) 40%
   d) _____?

3. Calculate the selling price on a job that has $1,751 in material costs, and $838.16 in labour costs (employee benefits included). Your overhead costs are 38%. What is your break-even price?

---

[39] (Note that direct labour costs, equipment rentals and material purchases are not part of overhead.)

a) $2,589.16
b) $3,573.04
c) $4,176 .06
d) $6,813.58
e) $_____?

4. You purchase a product for $10 and sell it to your customer for $15. You have just made:

a) 50% profit
b) 50% markup
c) 33% markup
d) 33% profit

5. You decide to purchase a machine that costs $35,000 (interest included). You have 500 hours of work for this machine per year and the machine should last 8 years before you would trade it in. Assume that the trade-in price will be $5,000. How much is the machine costing you per hour?

a) I paid cash for the machine, why should I charge for it?
b) Monthly payments divided by monthly use.
c) $15 per hour for the machine.
d) Going rate in the industry.
e) The machine should not be purchased because there is not enough work for it.

ANSWERS TO ESTIMATING QUIZ

Look at the answers below and evaluate where you stand. Remember, you should be scrutinizing your estimating skills with as much care as you would use when examining the execution of the work itself.

1. The answer is (c) $3,333.33. When you multiply $10,000 x 25%, you establish a markup of 25% (or $2,500) for a gross profit of only 20%.

The markup in dollars, $2,500, divided by the sales figure in dollars, ($12,500) equals 20% profit. To establish a real 25% profit, you calculate as follows:

$$\frac{\$10,000}{100\% - 25\%}$$

$$= \$13,333.33$$

2. The answer is (c) 40%. Your overhead is a direct comment on the kind of business you operate and includes all direct expenses from administration to utilities. It is interesting that larger companies have a lower overhead than smaller companies. This is extremely important for start-up companies.

3. The answer is (c) $4,176.06. Again, your direct cost of doing the job divided by your overhead:

$$\frac{\$1,751.00 + \$838.16}{100\% - 38\%}$$

$$= \$4,176.06[40]$$

---

[40] Once you establish your take-off costs, (Cost of Goods Sold) to do the job, you can calculate break-even with accuracy in front of the customer if necessary. Profit is calculated by dividing the break-even cost of the job by your desired profit less 100%. For example, 9% profit is (100% - 9%) = 91%. You would divide by 91 % to arrive at 9% profit!

4. The answer is (b) and (d), a 50% markup but only a 33% gross profit. Far too many contractors believe they have just made 50% profit. This single miscalculation is the downfall of many contractors. If your overhead is 35%, then this 50% markup allows you only 33% profit to apply toward your costs.

5. The answer is c) $15 per hour. When you decide to purchase equipment, you should consider the following:

- *How much do I have to charge per hour for the machine?*
- *Should I purchase or rent?*
- *How much should I charge per hour?*

The calculation is as follows:

$$\frac{\text{Total cost of machine}}{\text{(Lifespan of the machine divided by 2) x hours of use}}$$

$$\frac{\$35,000 - \$5,000.\text{ trade-in}}{\text{(8 years divided by 2) x 500 hours per year}}$$

= $15.00 per hour (your cost per hour for this machine)

- You divide the lifespan of the machine by 2 to ensure your return on investment.
- Over 8 years you will charge your customers $60,000 (or 8 years x 500 hours x $15.00)
- This enables you to pay off the machine and have funds available for the next purchase.
- To calculate the charge to the customer for this machine, you enter the cost per hour, $15.00, plus the cost of the employee who will drive it, including employee benefits.

$$\frac{\$15 + \$20 \text{ per hr } + 20\% \text{ benefits}}{100\% - \text{ Overhead of } 38\%}$$

$$\frac{\$39}{62\%}$$

$$= \$62.90$$

Note that you need to charge $62.90 just to break even, and we did not calculate for profit! Judge for yourself. Should you purchase, subcontract or rent this machine?

CHAPTER 7

PUBLIC WORKS RESTRUCTURING:[41]
USING YOUR LEVERAGE

7.1 POSITIVE RESTRUCTURING

The Public Works[42] system is inefficient and badly structured due to a very highly paid work force (50% higher than industry averages) that does not have to worry about job security. The pyramid system of job security, whereby management realizes that their own jobs are at risk unless they can create more jobs, is an enabling factor.

Fundamentally, privatization in this department would mean that the government would relinquish control of all public activities, including administration of operations and actual operations, and would sell off excess land, buildings and equipment.

A positive restructuring would enable existing staff (with the exception of the managing executives) presently performing these activities to continue to perform them as a private contractor company to the taxpayer.

Existing staff would be transformed to become self-employed companies. They would gain ownership of the applicable equipment (owned by the government departments, i.e. taxpayers at this time) and would be considered on a contractual basis for identical work being performed (i.e. no cutbacks in service) for a probationary period of five years.

---

[41] This chapter is based on a submission to the Fraser Institute which was presented to Municipal, Provincial and Federal levels of government. The article was awarded second place for this category. It is interesting to see that all levels of government are increasingly turning to the private sector to address escalating budgets and tax increases.

[42] This includes municipal, state, provincial and federal levels.

Additional work to be done, i.e. capital improvement, or work other than the daily routines of the present government employees, would be available for tender. This is essentially the same as it is today, with the exception that the newly formed employee-contractor company would have access to the tendering procedure in the same way as private sector companies have today.

7.2 THE TAX HEADACHE

Alarming tax increases have infuriated many taxpayers. They wonder how taxes got to be so outrageously high. Is it possible to lower costs without lowering employee morale? Saving $100,000 here and $100,000 there does not really get to the root of the problem and may cause a lot of frustration. A pill can relieve a headache, but in the long run, it may be more beneficial for the sufferer to find the cause of the headache and deal with that.

The cause of the tax headache is extremely high administrative and operational costs. In a democratic society that aims to serve its people, by the people, privatization makes sense for all.

HIGH ADMINISTRATIVE COSTS + HIGH OPERATING COSTS = TAX HEADACHE

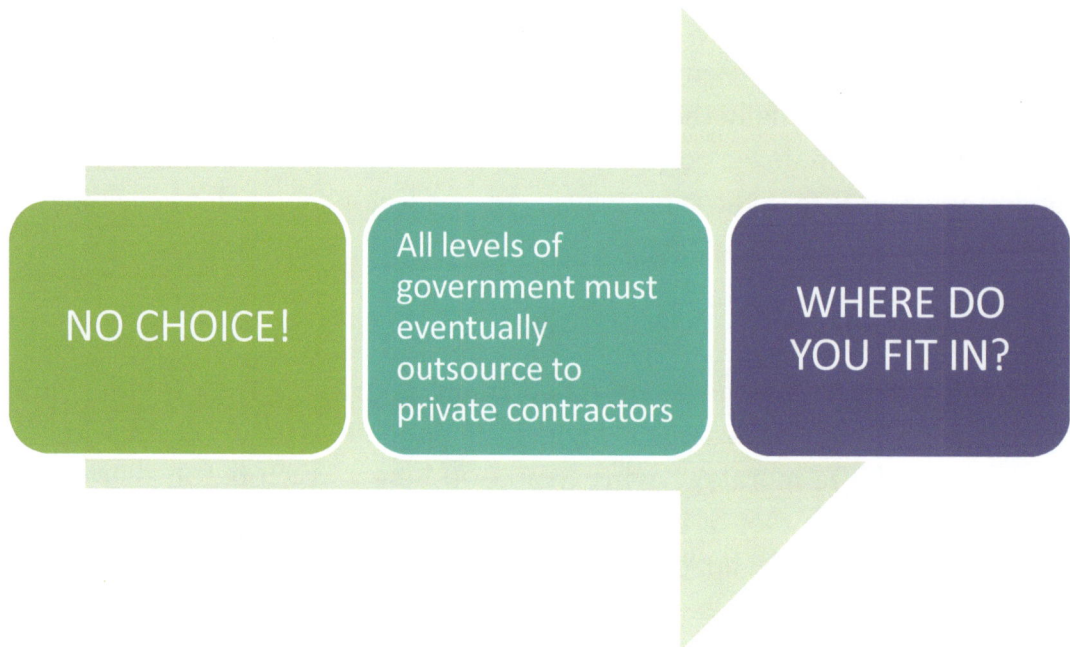

NO CHOICE! → **All levels of government must eventually outsource to private contractors** → **WHERE DO YOU FIT IN?**

7.3 PROBLEMS WITH THE PYRAMID SYSTEM OF JOB SECURITY

The Public Works system is inefficient and badly structured. The inefficiency and inadequately functioning structure is due to:

1. A very well-paid workforce (50% higher than industry averages) that does not have to worry about job security.
2. The pyramid system of job security
3. Management realizes that their own jobs are at risk unless they can create more jobs.
4. Departments have to negotiate for proper machinery, and 99% of the time they purchase the wrong machine for the job. This is due to budget restraints as a result of point #1 and point #2. Take a look at Fig. 7.1 and 7.2.

FIG. 7.1 "MAKE WORK" PROJECTS

- "Make work"-type projects such as cutting grass in parks, quash any possibilities for reforestation. Keeping employees and equipment busy "justifies" budget demands; environmental or naturalization projects do not, as they require fewer employees and equipment.
- As funds are not available for proper planning with respect to purchasing cost-efficient items that in the long run save money, money is wasted on less relatively expensive items that can increase the cost by tenfold.
- In City Parks and Recreation Departments, it is quite common to plant up a bed of annuals for the summer. With the arrival of the frost, annuals are pulled out and replaced with bulbs. This cycle is repeated every spring and fall.
- A cost-saving measure here would be to plant these beds with perennials or ground covers and leave the bulbs in the ground for naturalization. Initially, this procedure is more costly, but in the long run it saves a lot of money.

FIG. 7.2 PURCHASING THE WRONG EQUIPMENT

- Purchasing a 4-Wheel Drive pickup (gasoline) at a cost of $42,000 per pickup. This vehicle generally uses 17 litres to go 100 kilometres[43] at a cost of $1 per litre. Over a period of eight years this vehicle costs 14.63 cents per kilometre, based on 250,000 km of use (i.e. capital cost, maintenance, insurance and gas).
- A similar 2-Wheel Drive, at a cost of $30,000 would be much more efficient. This vehicle uses 10 litres of diesel fuel to go 100 kilometres at a cost of $1 per litre. Over the same eight year period, this vehicle costs 0.07 cents per kilometre. Maintenance costs can also be reduced by up to 20% due to the efficiency of diesel fuel. There are similar situations for dump trucks and lawn tractors.

---

[43] This would equal 25 miles per gallon.

4 WHEEL DRIVE TRUCK

Cost of vehicle is $42,000 less residual of $10,000 = $32,000	32,000
Gas	42,500
Maintenance	15,000
Insurance	10,000
Total	99,000 or 0.40 cents per kilometre

2 WHEEL DRIVE TRUCK

Cost of vehicle is $30,000 less residual of $5,000 = $25,000	25,000
Gas	25,000
Maintenance	8,000
Insurance	10,000
Total	68,000 or 0.27 cents per kilometre

7.4 HOW PRIVATIZATION WOULD BE INTRODUCED

A typical arrangement would be as follows: the equipment would be granted to the newly established "employee contractor company" at no cost, providing that certain conditions are met. See Fig. 7.3.

FIG. 7.3 RULES FOR EMPLOYEE CONTRACTOR COMPANIES

- The "employee-contractor company" performs all work to existing standards.
- The "employee-contractor company" reduces the cost of work by 4% annually during the five-year contract.
- The "employee-contractor company" completes the full five-year contract prior to gaining full ownership of the equipment involved. This would be covered by personal guarantees, and if necessary, liens on existing equipment and new purchases if they replace the equipment that is liened.

7.5 HOW THE GOVERNMENT WOULD EXERCISE A MONITORING ROLE

The remaining "managing executives" (who retain their present jobs in the government) would be responsible for necessary "employee-contractor company" meetings and standards, as well as supervising quality control.

- The "managing executives" would work with the newly formed "employee-contractor company" to see that all work is performed to the agreed norm and that any discrepancies or deficiencies are dealt with appropriately.
- All existing standards would be written up in a policy manual, agreed to by both parties.
- Conflicts would be resolved by a committee of industry experts, the union, the government and taxpayers.
- The "managing executives" would work with the newly formed "employee-contractor company" in the same manner as is currently the case with private sector companies.

7.6 FINANCIAL ASPECTS OF PRIVATIZATION

At this time, the average government employee earns $26.50 per hour plus employee benefits of approximately 30% for a total of $34.45 per hour. The average private sector employee earns $17.50 per hour plus employee benefits of 20% for a total of $21.00 per hour[44].

The remarkable contrast in employee costs is one matter. Overhead and indirect operating costs are more serious: The average private sector firm has an overhead of 35% to 40% while the larger companies can operate at 20% overhead.

Government overhead and indirect operating costs are approximately 50%. Overhead and indirect operating costs for the government are calculated on what it would cost taxpayers to do the job under the present system.

---

[44] Figures used are fictional.

This means that approximately 50% of the total budget is required to administer and manage the direct workforce.

When examined further, it is evident that there is a huge difference between the charge to the taxpayer per government employee hour vs. the private sector employee charge.

Take a look at Fig. 7.4 and 7.5.

FIG. 7.4 HOURLY RATE FOR A PRIVATE SECTOR EMPLOYEE

$$= \frac{\$17.50 \text{ per hour} + 20\% \text{ benefits}}{100\% - (\text{overhead of } 40\%)}$$

$$= \frac{\$21.00}{60\%}$$

$$= \$35.00 \text{ per hour}$$

FOR 10% PROFIT

$$= \frac{\$35.00}{100\% - 10\% \text{ profit}}$$

$$= \frac{\$35.00}{90\%}$$

$$= \$38.89 \text{ per hour}$$

FIG. 7.5 HOURLY RATE FOR AN AVERAGE GOVERNMENT EMPLOYEE

$$\frac{\$26.50 \text{ per hour} + 30\% \text{ benefits}}{100\% - (50\% \text{ overhead})}$$

$$= \frac{\$34.45}{50\%}$$

$$\$68.90 \text{ per hour}$$

The difference in costs to the taxpayer works out to: $68.90 - $38.89 = $30.01 per hour.

7.7 SPECIFICATIONS OF COST SAVINGS FOR THE TAXPAYER

In the case of all competing private contractors, "downtime" is charged back into the formula:

Downtime:

$$\frac{\$17.50 \text{ per hour} + 20\% \text{ benefits}}{100\% - 20\% \text{ downtime}}$$

$$= \frac{\$21.00}{80\%}$$

$26.25 per hour

7.8 CHARGE PER HOUR FOR A PRIVATE SECTOR EMPLOYEE

To get the correct charge per hour for a private sector employee (including downtime, overhead and profit) calculate as shown in Fig. 7.6.

In the case of the government employee, "downtime" is generally more than 25%. The industry standard is about 20% for a variety of reasons (including coffee breaks and travel).

FIG. 7.6 CHARGE PER HOUR FOR PRIVATE SECTOR EMPLOYEE

$$\frac{\textbf{Employee cost per hour (including downtime)}}{\textbf{100\% } - \textbf{ Overhead \%}}$$

$$= \frac{\$26.25}{100\% - 40\%}$$

$$= \frac{\$26.25}{60\%}$$

$$= \$43.75 \text{ per hour}$$

FOR 10% PROFIT

$$\frac{\$43.75}{100\% - 10\% \text{ profit}}$$

$$= \$48.61 \text{ per hour}$$

7.9 GOVERNMENT EMPLOYEE COSTS PER HOUR

The government employee costs per hour to the taxpayer are calculated as shown in Fig. 7.7. This includes downtime.

The true charge to the taxpayer per government employee hour (including overhead and profit) vs. the private sector is as follows:

$91.86 for public sector vs. $48.61 for private sector

FIG. 7.7 COST PER HOUR TO TAXPAYER

$$\frac{\$26.50 \text{ per hour} + 30\% \text{ benefits}}{100\% - 25\% \text{ down time}}$$

$$= \frac{\$34.45}{75\%}$$

$$= \$45.93 \text{ per hour}$$

To establish break-even[45]

$$\frac{\$45.93}{100\% - \text{overhead } \%}$$

$$\frac{\$45.93}{100\% - 50\%}$$

$$\frac{\$45.93}{50\%}$$

$$= \$91.86 \text{ per hour}$$

All things being equal, what effect will the difference have on the taxpayer bill?

7.10 EMPLOYEE CONTRACTOR COMPANY VS. PRIVATE SECTOR COMPANIES

With respect to what the taxpayer would have to pay, the difference is: $91.86 per hour per government employee vs. $48.61 per hour per competing private contractor employee. In each case, "overhead costs" include equipment costs and maintenance, management costs, administration costs, land and buildings. The need for large offices, garages, buildings and property owned by the taxpayer would be decreased, in turn allowing money to be freed up for capital projects.

---

[45] Since government departments are not for profit.

7.11 SAVINGS

What is the solution? Let's suppose that the Government gave up *direct* responsibility in favour of *governing* a privately run *employee-contractor company*. It is quite possible that an immediate and substantial reduction to existing government overhead would occur.[46]

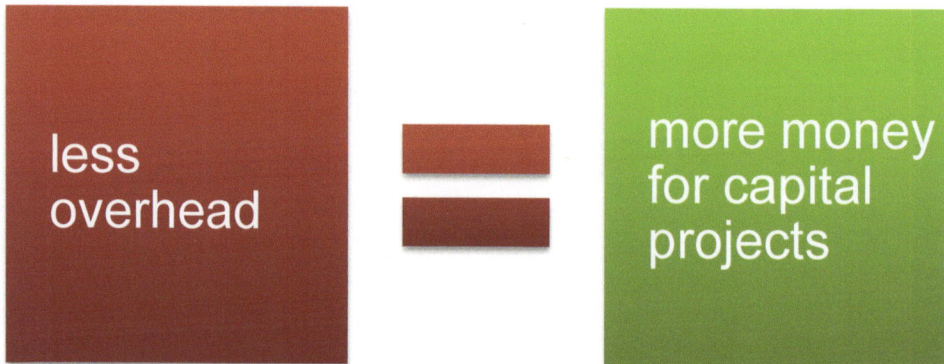

less overhead = more money for capital projects

The new reduced government overhead costs[47] are added to the hourly rate of the newly established *employee contractor companies* as per the formula outlined above.

With respect to the taxpayer, using the 10% government overhead, this affects the hourly rate of the *employee contractor company in* the following manner. See Fig. 7.8.

---

[46] And therefore, cost to the taxpayer.
[47] Government no longer has the same overhead costs.

FIG. 7.8 HOW THE HOURLY RATE IS AFFECTED

New employee hourly rate: $17.50
Employee benefits: 20%

DOWNTIME

$$\frac{\$17.50 \text{ per hour} + \$3.50 \text{ benefits}}{100\% - \text{Downtime } 20\%}$$

$$= \frac{\$21.00}{80\%}$$

$$= \$26.25$$

BREAK-EVEN

$$\frac{\$17.50 \text{ per person hour (plus benefits} + \text{ downtime)}}{100\% - (\text{overhead of } 40\% + \text{Government overhead of } 10\%)}$$

$$\frac{\$26.25}{100\% - (40\% \text{ overhead} + 10\% \text{ government overhead})}$$

$$= \frac{\$26.25}{50\%}$$

$$= \$52.50$$

PROFIT

$$\frac{\$52.50}{100\% - 10\% \text{ profit}}$$

$$= \frac{\$52.50}{90\%}$$

$$= \$58.33 \text{ per hour}$$

7.12 TRUE SAVINGS

The true savings then, should equal approximately the difference between the present $58.33 per *"employee contractor company"* government hour and the $$91.86 government public sector employee cost.[48]

The result is a saving of $33.53 per working hour.

These savings have the potential to grow annually as the newly established *"employee contractor company"* could be committed to reducing the hourly charge by 4% per hour per year.

7.13 RESTRUCTURING

The restructuring would eliminate equipment and maintenance costs to the taxpayer. Building costs would be reduced by 50% or more due to the abandoning of most premises for smaller and more feasible premises.

Excess land and buildings may be rented out to the *"employee contractor company"* or sold off completely. The government overhead and indirect operational costs would drop to 10% of the employee costs indicated above.

This restructuring would not merely save taxpayers in the first year, but for an additional four years. After that, each job would be subject to the open tendering process, with the possibility of additional savings for the government.

Look at the example on the next page.

---

[48] Government administration and management are included.

FIG. 7.9 USING THE PRIVATIZATION SYSTEM (AN EXAMPLE)

- If a certain type of government job requires 8 hours, then under the new privatization system, the same job would be paid for the equivalent 8 hours
- If the *employee-contractor company* is able to do the same job in less than 8 hours while meeting existing standards, then s/he will have additional time to pursue other work, i.e. increase earning potential.

7.14 NEW CORPORATE TAXPAYERS

Privatized *"employee-contractor companies"* would be able to do additional work, over and above their duties as prescribed for them in return for the government contract.

Under the right management system, these *"employee-contractor companies"* would earn sufficient return on investment to purchase new equipment outright as well as earn a 10% profit per year. The *"employee-contractor companies"* would become new corporate taxpayers and have more control of and pride in their work.

To ensure that these new *"employee-contractor companies"* do not disintegrate after the five-year period, the tendering process would demand that competing companies pay their workers the same hourly rate as the newly privatized *"employee-contractor companies"* for the duration of the contract. Unionization could also be the norm.

7.15 OBSTACLES TO BE OVERCOME AND RECOMMENDATIONS

The only real obstacle to be overcome is the fear of the present government worker with regard to losing an accepted standard of security that has been taken for granted.

7.16 BENEFITS FOR TAXPAYERS AND EMPLOYEES

If this proposal is adopted, it may be considered a win-win situation for all concerned. There are benefits for the government, for taxpayers and for employees.

- Unions would be able to retain membership and ensure existing employee safety standards.
- Government workers would regain control and would be able to share in the new privatization venture.
- New *"employee contractor companies"* would be able to actively participate in job security and profit sharing.
- Existing pay and benefits levels would be maintained.
- Taxpayers would be relieved to see that tax bills are not increased and that savings are used to invest in capital projects and to maintain and improve the infrastructure.
- All parties would be interested in capital works projects that save time and money in the future.
- Newly formed *"employee-contractor companies,"* in agreeing to reduce costs by 4% per hour to taxpayers, would reduce costs if workload diminishes.
- Existing government managers/administration would retain functions and expertise in order to build and improve infrastructure and services, as opposed to stripping them.
- Within five years, taxpayer costs of the public works department would be cut in half.

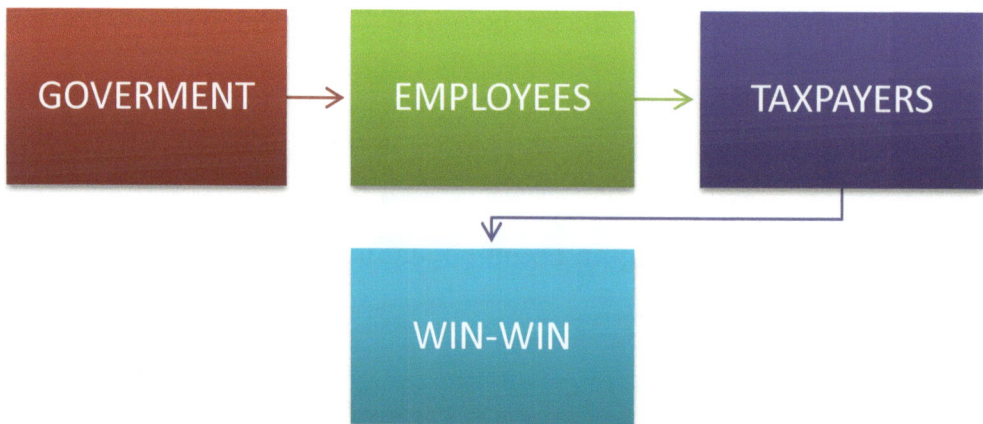

```
GOVERMENT  →  EMPLOYEES  →  TAXPAYERS
                                 ↓
                             WIN-WIN
```

CONCLUSION

If proven in a "test case" for the public works department, this system could be tried with other sectors of the government. On the other hand, if this proposal (or a similar one) is not implemented in the near future, then many government employees will face layoffs as services are cut back in response to government attempts to cut costs. In that bleak scenario, everyone suffers, and our infrastructure may deteriorate at an ever accelerating rate.

CHAPTER 8

PRICING PER SQUARE FOOT AND WHY THIS FAILS YOU: IT'S SIMPLE AND STUPID

8.1 WHAT DO YOU CHARGE PER SQUARE FOOT?

The telephone rings. A customer has just called to enquire about your "price per square foot" to install an interlock driveway. Although consumers expect to be given a price per square foot, and many contractors believe it is possible to price this way, in reality it is impossible to do this type of pricing over the telephone.

Companies vary widely in how they execute their work. Companies differ in the amount of overhead they have. Why then, does unit pricing continue to be used by so many landscaping companies?

Let's take a look at a sample driveway job. Here are the specifications:

- Dimensions of the rectangular driveway are 20 feet wide by 50 feet long.
- Excavation requirements to a depth of 12 inches.
- Material: We will use rectangular interlocking stones.
- Procedure: We will snap-edge the two longer sides and fill the joints with polymer sand.
- Finishing: Repairs to the grass and a general clean up are mandatory.

8.2 METHODOLOGY

What methodology should be used to do this job? To start, we will have the driveway excavated and backfilled by a subcontractor.

In my experience, subcontractors in many regions will execute this work for $1,000 to $1,250. Specifically, this means that the subcontractor will dig out the driveway, dispose of the excavated material and backfill with 3/4 crusher run. The price may be a little higher in larger urban areas.

We estimate that it will take three employees 12 hours (one work day) to complete this work as specified above. This includes the following:

- Levelling and compacting
- Cutting and laying the stone
- Snap edging
- Polymer sand
- Repairs and cleanup

Actual prices will vary from one area to another. We will use the above figures for our analysis. Take a look at Fig. 8.1 to 8.3 for a breakdown of material and labour costs for this job.

FIG. 8.1 BREAK DOWN OF MATERIAL COSTS[49]

MATERIAL	PRICE PER UNIT	TOTAL
20 yards 3/4 crushed run	$67.00	$1,340.00*
6 tons limestone screening	$50.00	$300.00*
1000 sq. ft. rect. interlock	$2.65/sq. ft.	$2,650.00*
100 linear ft. aluminum snap edge	8' strips + nails	$230.00 + $30.00
10 bags polymer sand	$30	$300.00
Soil and seed	1/2 screened yard soil + 1 bag seed	$40.00 + $30.00
Total Material		$4,920.00

---

[49] The figures shown in this table are not necessarily current. They are intended to give an example of material cost breakdown. Note that taxes are not included.

*Delivery included.

FIG. 8.2 BREAK DOWN OF LABOUR COSTS

EMPLOYEE	WAGES/HOUR
Foreperson	$20.00
Second employee	$17.50
Third employee	$16.00
Total hourly rate	$53.50

FIG. 8.3 TOTAL LABOUR COSTS FOR THIS JOB

HOURLY RATE	TIME NEEDED	EMPLOYEE BENEFITS	TOTAL LABOUR COST
$53.50	12 Hours (1 day)	20%	$770.40

8.3 ADDING PROFIT TO THE SUBCONTRACTOR PRICE

Take the subcontractor price shown in section 8.2 and add your desired profit to this figure. In this case, we are looking for a 20% profit:

$$\frac{\$1,250}{100\% - \text{desired profit percentage } (20\%)}$$

$$= \frac{\$1,250}{80\%}$$

$$= \$1,562.50$$

We will then add this $1,562.50 to our price for the job which will include labour, materials and overhead.

Once we have our final pricing, we can then divide by the area of 1,000 square feet and establish our unit price per square foot.

This is where contractors vary widely in price and methodology. Of the companies that I have examined, many have indicated that this type of job would take two days.

Other contractors prefer to do the excavation work themselves. Some contractors want to cut the stones individually, while others cut in one line.

In addition to materials and labour, we need to calculate for overhead. A benchmark landscape company has an overhead of 32%; however, the industry average is approximately 40%.

For our example here, we will propose that the contractor can get the job completed in one day[50] and requires $5,690.40 or $5.69 per square foot just to cover costs. Take a look at the calculation below.

CATEGORY	$ COSTS
Materials	4,920.00
Labour	770.40
TOTAL	5,690.40

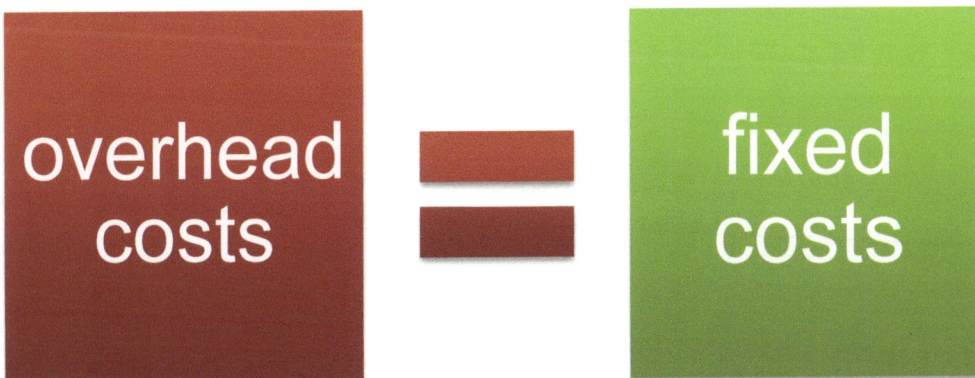

overhead costs = fixed costs

---

50 Provided that excavation has been completed and backfill is in place.

To break even, calculate as follows:

$$\frac{\$4,920.00 + \$770.40}{100\% - 32\% \text{ (overhead)}}$$

$$= \frac{\$5,690.40}{68\%}$$

$$= \$8,368$$

Or $8.37 per square foot

For a contractor with a 40% overhead the calculation would be:

$$\frac{\$4920.00 + \$770.40}{100\% - 40\% \text{ (overhead)}}$$

$$= \frac{\$5,690.40}{60\%}$$

$$= \$9.484$$

or: $9.48 per square foot

8.4 WHAT THE MARKET WILL "BARE"

What will the market accept as the square foot price? Since regions vary, prices will fluctuate accordingly.

Are there variables that can be adjusted to your advantage?

If you change the dimensions to 40 feet by 80 feet or 3,200 square feet, the job could now take three days to complete, resulting in higher subcontractor charges, but not 3.2 times the 1,000 square foot driveway price, and materials will remain the same on a square foot basis. You will be installing a 3,200 square feet driveway in three days vs. a 1,000 square foot driveway in one day.

Remember, overhead costs are fixed costs,[51] and it is difficult to link these to unit pricing. It is impossible to be exact with unit pricing, and this pricing method should be avoided, at all costs.

Therefore, in theory you could charge less per square foot as the job grows in size. However, if you had a set charge of (for example) $10 per square foot, you would become uncompetitive. This is where pricing per square foot really lets you down.

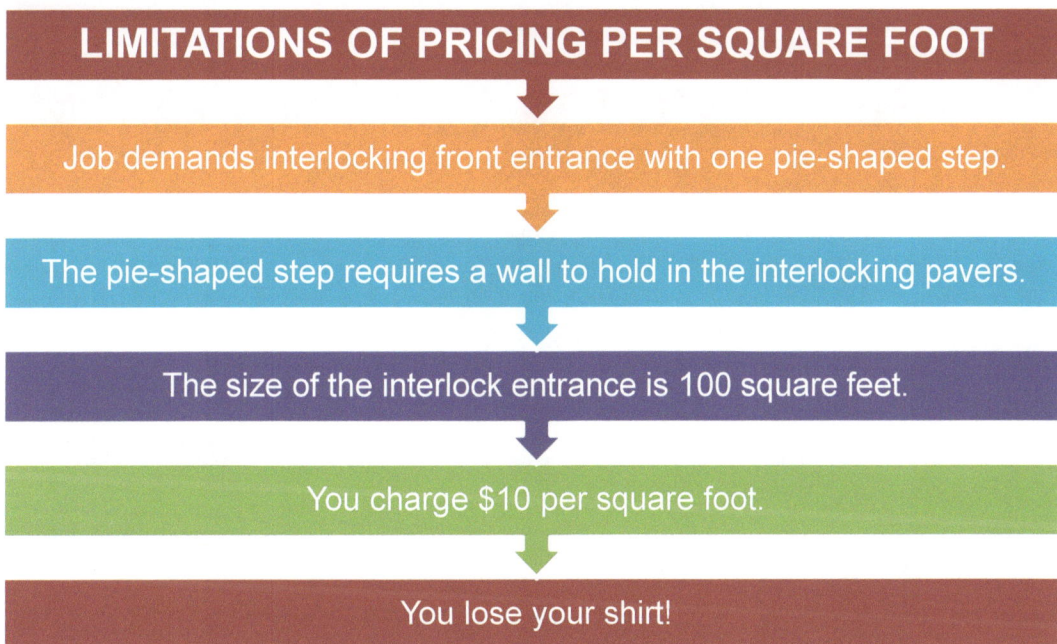

LIMITATIONS OF PRICING PER SQUARE FOOT

Job demands interlocking front entrance with one pie-shaped step.

The pie-shaped step requires a wall to hold in the interlocking pavers.

The size of the interlock entrance is 100 square feet.

You charge $10 per square foot.

You lose your shirt!

Some time ago, I actually completed a job similar to the one in this example. Can you guess what the "per square foot price" was? The answer is $40 per square foot and $600 extra for the wall. This job required a tremendous amount of cutting, and because the job was a "small job" only two employees were engaged. Note that to complete this job, two employees worked two full 12-hour days.

---

[51] Indirect costs.

PLANTING JOBS USING FACTORS OF 2 OR MORE

Oddly enough, I still see many companies who charge by square foot or by linear foot. Worse, some companies price planting jobs at 2 times, 2.5 times, 3 times or 3.5 times the cost of the plant! There is an advantage to using this method when quoting. It is possible to calculate your price very quickly.

Similarly, many companies estimate using their "numbers" so that they can automatically deliver a "break-even" price. Both systems are inaccurate.

The chart below demonstrates what happens when companies charge the price of the plant times "x" for a plant installation job.

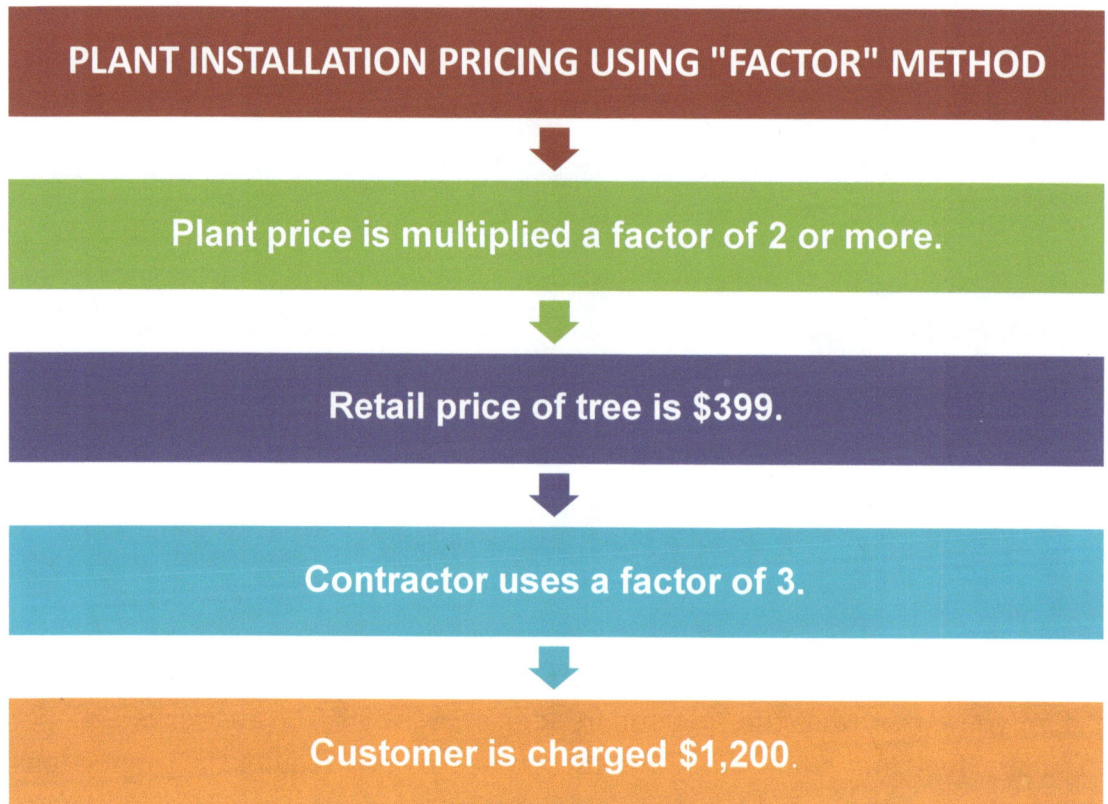

PLANT INSTALLATION PRICING USING "FACTOR" METHOD
⬇
Plant price is multiplied a factor of 2 or more.
⬇
Retail price of tree is $399.
⬇
Contractor uses a factor of 3.
⬇
Customer is charged $1,200.

A more accurate way to estimate is shown in Fig. 8.4.

FIG. 8.4.	
MATERIALS	**$ COST**
Price of tree ($399 less 25%)	299.00
Tree stake and wires	14.00
5 bags soil	25.00
1 bag mulch	10.00
Bone meal/transplanter-starter	10.00
TOTAL MATERIALS	**358.00**
LABOUR	
2 EMPLOYEES X 4 HOURS = 8 HOURS Pick up tree and materials, excavate, plant tree, return to shop and disposals)	
Foreman (4 hours x $20) = $80	
Second (4 hours x $16) = $64	
Payroll tax 20% = $28.80	
Downtime = 0	
TOTAL WAGES	**172.80**

Using Fig. 8.4, we would establish "break-even" as follows:

$$\frac{\text{Materials} + \text{labour}}{100\% - \text{your overhead percentage}}$$

$$\frac{\$358. + \$172.80}{100\% - \text{your overhead of } 40\%}$$

$$\frac{\$530.80}{60\%}$$

$$\$884.67$$

Wow! You could actually do this tree planting job at "break-even" for $884.67! However, you still need to provide a warranty and allow for a fair profit of 20% as well as a replacement charge of 10% minimum.

FINAL PRICE MUST INCLUDE

Profit

Warranty

Replacement costs

Therefore, your price to your customer should include your break-even cost with a proper markup for profit and replacement. Look at the calculation below:

$$\frac{\text{Break-even cost}}{100\% - (\text{your desired profit and replacement cost})}$$

$$\frac{\$884.67}{100\% - (20\% \text{ profit} + 10\% \text{ replacement cost})}$$

$$\frac{\$884.67}{70\%}$$

$$\$1,263.81$$

So there you have it! Pricing using the simple method would result in a price of $1,200 as opposed to $1,263.81 using our more accurate system. What is $63.81? Perhaps this does not seem that significant, but if we carry this amount forward throughout the course of the year, this difference can really add up. This was an example using just one tree. What if you were planting 10 trees? Using this factor system would eventually price you out of the job.

Let's take a closer look.

FIG. 8.5.	
MATERIALS	**$ COST**
Using Fig. 8.4, material costs would multiplied by 10[52] ($358. X 10) Note that you could use bulk soil instead of bags to save money.	3,580.00
TOTAL MATERIALS	**3,580.00**
LABOUR 5 EMPLOYEES + MINI EXCAVATOR (Depending on the placement of the trees and accessibility, it is possible to plant 10 trees in 5 hours with a well-organized team.) Foreman (5 hours x $20) = $100 Second (5 hours x $16) = $80 Third (5 hours x $15) = $75 Fourth (5 hours x $14) = $70 Fifth (5 hours x $14) = $70 Payroll tax 20% = $79.00 Downtime = 0 Disposal costs = 0	
TOTAL WAGES	474.00

[52] Ten trees vs. cost of one.

Note that in this example, equipment and vehicle expenses are included in the 40% overhead. For break-even cost:

$$\text{Total material cost and total labour cost} \over \text{100\% - your overhead cost}$$

$$= \frac{\$3,580 + \$474}{100\% - 40\%}$$

$$\frac{\$474}{60\%}$$

$$= \$6,756.67 \text{ break-even}$$

FOR PROFIT AND REPLACEMENT COST:

$$\text{Break-even cost} \over \text{100\% - (your desired profit \% + replacement cost)}$$

$$= \frac{\$6,756.67}{100\% - (20\% \text{ profit} + 10\% \text{ replacement cost})}$$

$$= \frac{\$6,756.67}{70\%}$$

$$= \$9,652.39$$

$$\$9,652.39 \div 10 \text{ trees} = \$965.24 \text{ per tree}$$

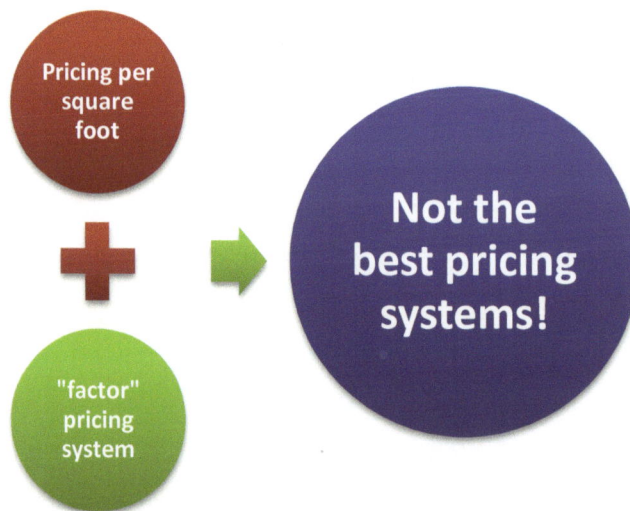

Pricing per square foot

+

→

Not the best pricing systems!

"factor" pricing system

CHAPTER 9

SNOW REMOVAL PRICING:
HOW TO LOSE MONEY IN SNOW

9.1 CHANGES IN THE SNOW REMOVAL BUSINESS

When I started a snow removal operation in 1976, this business service was undergoing massive change. Back then, hand-operated blowers were the norm for clearing snow from driveways. This was both time consuming and very wet, uncomfortable work.

That year, I decided to go another route and purchased snow blades for our vehicles. This was considered quite a big move at the time, but the results were immediate and quite astonishing. By modernizing our equipment, our productivity increased tremendously. We were now able to accomplish three times the work in the same period. And we stayed dry!

But there was a downside. While output increased, prices started to go down. Unfortunately, snow removal companies who did not modernize could not compete and were soon out of business. Customers benefited because snow removal prices remained practically unchanged for over 30 years.

Once again, the snow removal business is changing, and there seems to be a close parallel to the situation in 1976. Snow removal with the blade system is quickly being replaced by tractors with snow blowers.

While it is possible to increase productivity and accomplish three times the work in the same time frame, unfortunately, there is a corresponding downward turn in pricing. Those companies who cannot afford to adapt to changing situations will not likely survive the next five years.

9.2 SHOULD YOU REMAIN IN THIS BUSINESS?

Companies do snowplowing for these reasons:

- Cash flow.
- To keep their employees employed, for fear of losing them.
- To keep their summer maintenance customers happy.
- For the salting contracts.
- Snow removal is the main core of their business.

Do these companies know the true cost of doing snow removal? Should these companies remain in this business? In my experience, I have seen that snow removal is not for all companies.

Let us examine what it really means to stay in the snow removal business. The cost to these companies needs to be closely examined. We will also explore actual snow removal costs in this chapter.

FIG. 9.1 SNOW REMOVAL VS "NO REMOVAL"

- A snow removal company needs a 4x4 truck to remove snow.
- A "no removal company" can operate using a 2-wheel drive, six cylinder. This costs less than half the price of the 4x4!
- Gas, insurance, repairs and utilities cost twice as much for a "snow removal company" compared to what they would be for a "no removal" company.
- "No removal" companies require less equipment and storage space. They do not need a shop to make repairs and adjustments.
- Insurance costs are becoming prohibitive, and the direct as well as indirect cost to the contractor must be considered.

9.3 WHERE DOES OVERHEAD FIT IN?

It is very important to realize that every company has overhead to operate a business. A benchmark maintenance company will have an overhead of 42% during the course of the year.

Overhead is made up of every indirect cost from administration to utilities and includes gas, insurance and repairs as well as return on investment for vehicles and equipment. Obviously, there are extra costs involved when a company engages in snow removal work. Snow removal has fluctuating costs, which can cause total overhead to be higher than normal.

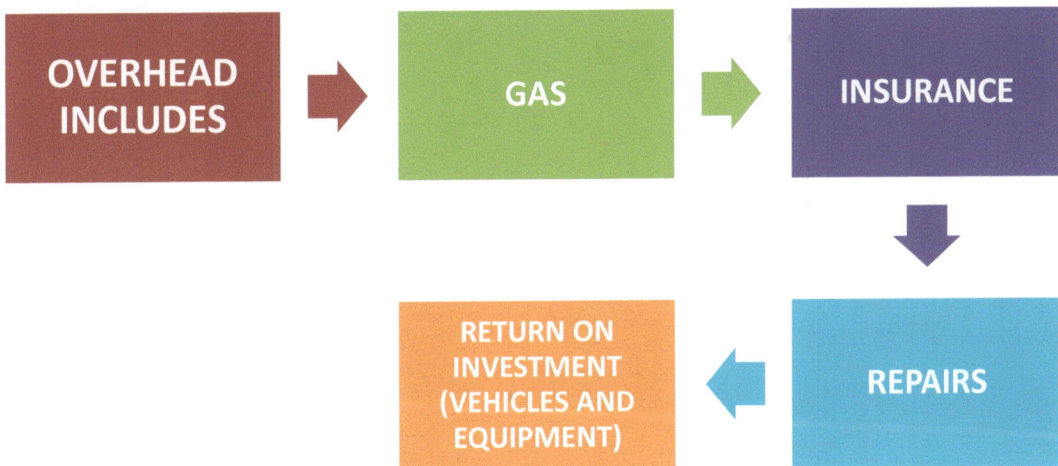

```
┌──────────────┐      ┌──────────────┐      ┌──────────────┐
│  OVERHEAD    │  ▶   │    GAS       │  ▶   │  INSURANCE   │
│  INCLUDES    │      │              │      │              │
└──────────────┘      └──────────────┘      └──────────────┘
                                                    │
                                                    ▼
      ┌──────────────┐                      ┌──────────────┐
      │ RETURN ON    │                      │              │
      │ INVESTMENT   │  ◀                   │   REPAIRS    │
      │ (VEHICLES AND│                      │              │
      │ EQUIPMENT)   │                      │              │
      └──────────────┘                      └──────────────┘
```

In theory, a company should have individual budgets for summer maintenance and winter maintenance. Each department has its own separate costs, and having this information available helps a company stay *competitive in each department*.

Many companies have a single budget for the year. This means that when they are engaged in summer maintenance jobs, they are actually charging all their customers the costs of the snow operation as well. Obviously, their overhead is that much higher.

To see how snow removal costs can affect your summer maintenance pricing, take a look at the case study below.

FIG. 9.2 CASE STUDY: WHAT IS INCLUDED IN THE PRICE?

ABC Maintenance charges Mr. Jones a certain price for summer property maintenance. Included in the price (though not explicit) is the following:

- 4x4 truck
- snow blade
- salter
- double repair cost
- double gas cost
- additional insurance costs
- additional "snow insurance" costs

Just imagine if you could be "lean and mean" in the summer and concentrate on productivity. It would be possible to generate 12 months of income in 8 months!

9.4 KEEPING EMPLOYEES

If employees want to work in winter, it is possible to pay them on a salary basis, by working more hours than normal in the summer. In other words, they would do a full year's worth of hours in eight to nine months and earn enough money to be paid a weekly salary during the winter months.

In order to get this premium, workers would have to work six days a week or 57.5 hours per week for 35 weeks. This would work out to approximately 2,000 hours, or a year's worth of work hours! If employees were paid 40 hours per week, then they could be paid all year.

FIG. 9.3 BREAK-EVEN HOURLY RATE FORMULA

$$\frac{Cost\ of\ Goods\ Sold}{100\% - Overhead\ \%}$$

$$\frac{Hourly\ rate\ +\ Payroll\ Tax}{100\% - your\ Overhead\ \%}$$

$$= \frac{\$25.00\ x\ 20\%\ (\$5.00)}{100\% - 42\%}$$

$$= \frac{\$30.00}{58\%}$$

$$= \$51.72\ break\text{-}even$$

9.5 WHAT ARE THE OPTIONS?

If you are in the snow removal business, you may want to explore some of the ideas outlined above. Consider these possibilities:

- Go into snow removal in a big way
- Subcontract all or part of your snow contracts
- Become more competitive and make more money so that you do not have to do snow removal!

Many companies are taking the last option very seriously and are working towards that goal.

9.6 CASE STUDY: COMMERCIAL EQUIPMENT

The following case study is an example of doing snow removal for cash flow. This is the scenario. You have 40 driveway contracts priced at $250 each, for a total revenue of $10,000, and it is necessary to clear driveways 20 to 25 times per season. It takes you or your driver 10 hours each time to set up, clear the snow, return and refit. This means that:

- You or your driver work between 20 to 25 times at 10 hours per time, for a total of 200 to 250 hours.
- At your break-even rate of $51.72 per hour, you have to charge $10,344 for 200 hours or $12,930 for 250 hours.
- Your revenue was $10,000.
- At $10,344 in total costs, you covered all expenses, i.e. labour and overhead.
- There is no profit.
- This is a poor example of doing snow removal for cash flow![53]
- You are actually losing money.

9.7 INDIVIDUAL PRICING FOR SNOW REMOVAL

This refers to pricing snow removal "by each time," and for this service, the client expects an hourly rate quotation for salting and sanding.

Some clients may expect a per time charge instead of an hourly rate. As in all snow removal situations, it is impossible to determine how many times it will be necessary to go out.

We will assume that:

- It takes 15 minutes to complete snow clearing for an average snowfall of 6 inches (15 cm).
- You will need to "guesstimate" the number of times you will be out per snow season.

---

[53] Imagine the situation if you went out 25 times.

FIG. 9.4 PRICE PER TIME AND DRIVER COSTS

If the average is 25 times per snow season, then the price per time for this service is calculated as follows:

SERVICE	AMOUNT
Driver	$25
Payroll taxes	20%
Downtime	25%
Overhead	42%
Expected profit	20%
Time to do job (segment)	15 minutes

To determine the cost of the driver, you must first determine what the driver costs including downtime. Use the *JPL Downtime Formula* as shown in Fig. 9.5.

FIG. 9.5 JPL DOWNTIME FORMULA

$$\frac{\textbf{Hourly rate} + \textbf{20\% Payroll Tax}}{\textbf{100\%} - \textbf{Downtime \%}}$$

$$= \frac{\$25.00 + \$5.00}{100\% - 25\%}$$

$$= \frac{\$30.00}{75\%}$$

$$= \$40.00$$

Now that we know that the driver costs $40 per hour, it is possible to figure out the charge to the client.

9.8 CHARGE TO THE CLIENT

To arrive at the charge to the client, use the *JPL Estimating Formula for Break-even*. Look at Fig. 9.6.

FIG. 9.6 JPL ESTIMATING FORMULA FOR BREAK-EVEN

$$\frac{\text{Hourly rate} + 20\% \text{ payroll tax}}{100\% - \text{Your Overhead }\%}$$

$$= \frac{\$40.00}{100\% - 42\%}$$

$$= \frac{\$40.00}{58\%}$$

$$= \$68.97 \text{ per hour}[54]$$

$$= \$17.24 \text{ per 15 minute increment}$$

You can now inform the client that it will cost $17.24 per time to clear the driveway. Remember this is your break-even cost. The calculation is as follows:

$68.97 ÷ 4 (15 minutes)

---

[54] This is break-even pricing.

This covers all your overhead expenses, (including fuel, insurances, repairs, etc.); however, this is break-even per hour pricing.

To make a 20% profit on this job, you would take the $68.97 per hour, and divide by 80% (100% - your desired profit of 20%).

Look at the formula shown in Fig. 9.7.

FIG. 9.7 JPL ESTIMATING FORMULA FOR BREAK-EVEN

$$\frac{\text{Break-even charge rate}}{100\% - 20\% \text{ desired profit}}$$

$$\$68.97 \div 4 \ (15 \text{ minutes})$$

$$= \frac{\$17.24}{80\%}$$

$$= \$21.55 \text{ per 15 minute increment}$$

Now you can tell your client that it takes 15 minutes to do the driveway each time at a rate of $21.55 per time. This is actually cheaper than the lawn maintenance rate!

9.9 INCREASING REVENUE WITH SALTING AND SANDING SERVICES

While snow removal is a very competitive business, it is possible to increase revenues by offering salting and sanding services.

To figure out how much to charge for salting and sanding, you need to know your costs.

Here are some key factors.

- Salt and sand should be purchased by the ton to get the best price.
- A price of approximately $80 per ton is considered normal.
- If you were to spread one ton of salt in one hour, you would be able to determine your hourly charge for this service. Normally, this service can be completed in less than one hour.
- Hourly wage and benefits to the driver.
- Down-time[55] is the time spent loading and unloading, as well as travel time to and from the site.
- Total cost of goods sold = down-time and materials.

9.10 CHARGING BY THE HOUR

Let us assume the following:

- It takes you 20 minutes to drive to and from the sand/salt depot.
- You drive to three sites with your load.
- Total travel time is 30 minutes.
- It takes you 10 minutes to spread the mixture at each client location.
- You require a total of one hour to complete the total job.

Your customer wants to be charged by the hour. How much should you charge for your services, knowing that it only takes 15 minutes to service the customer and only one-third of the salt per customer?

This means that your driver costs you $40 to do the job.

To determine the cost for the customer, incorporate this cost into the *JPL formula*.

If you were able to complete three jobs in one hour, your worker would cost you $60 per time for salting services.

---

[55] Downtime is very high in the snow removal business. The benchmark for lawn maintenance is 20% and for snow/salting services it is 40%. Having your own salt bins can decrease this downtime significantly.

To establish your break-even price to do this, calculate as shown in Fig. 9.8.

FIG. 9.8 JPL ESTIMATING FORMULA FOR BREAK-EVEN (CUSTOMER COST)

$$\frac{\text{Hourly rate for driver of } \$25. + 20\% \text{ Payroll Taxes}}{100\% \; - 50\% \text{ downtime}}$$

$$= \frac{\$30.00}{50\%}$$

$$= \$60.00$$

BREAK-EVEN FORMULA

$$\frac{\text{Cost of Goods Sold}}{100\% \; - \; \text{Overhead }\%}$$

$$\frac{\$60. \,(\text{wages}) + \; \$80. \,(\text{salt})}{100\% \; - \; 42\% \text{ overhead}}$$

$$= \frac{\$140.00}{58\%}$$

$$= \$241.38 \text{ to service 3 drops or jobs}$$

The break-even price to service three drops or jobs is therefore $241.38. To make a profit of 20% use the formula shown in Fig. 9.9.

FIG. 9.9 JPL ESTIMATING FORMULA (FOR PROFIT OF 20%)

$$\frac{\$241.38}{100\% \; - \; \text{your desired profit of } 20\%}$$

$$= \frac{\$241.38}{80\%}$$

$$= \$301.72$$

Or: $100.57 per customer

9.11 COST AND RETURN ON INVESTMENT (SNOW BLADE)

What happens when we use a snow blade?

- A snow blade adds another component to the equation.
- The snow blade is considered as equipment and is rented out on a per hour basis.

Enter the cost of the blade into the *JPL Equipment Costing Formula*. What is the true cost of a snow blade? Look at Fig. 9.10.

FIG. 9.10 TRUE COST OF A SNOW BLADE	
Gross cost of blade	$6,000
Lifespan	4 years
Residual value[56]	$1,000
Net cost of blade	$5,000

Now look at the *JPL Equipment Costing Formula* shown in Fig. 9.11.

FIG. 9.11 JPL ESTIMATING FORMULA (FOR PROFIT OF 20%)

$$\frac{\$5,000}{(\text{Lifespan} \div 2) \times \text{usage}}$$

$$= \frac{\$5,000}{(4 \div 2) \times 10 \text{ hours} \times 50 \text{ visits}^{[57]}}$$

$$= \frac{\$5,000}{2 \times 500} = \frac{\$5,000}{1,000}$$

$$= \$5.00 \text{ per hour}^{[58]}$$

---

[56] What you would sell this piece of equipment for at the end of its lifespan?
[57] Includes salting trips
[58] You are returning ROI to yourself at $5 per hour.

9.12 COST AND RETURN ON INVESTMENT (4X4 TRUCK - WINTER USE ONLY)

A 4x4 vehicle adds another element. The vehicle is considered as equipment and is rented back to you on a per hour basis. Put the cost of the vehicle into the JPL Equipment Costing Formula. What is the true cost of this 4x4 vehicle? Take a look at Fig. 9.12.

FIG. 9.12 TRUE COST OF A 4X4 VEHICLE[59] (WINTER USE ONLY)	
Gross cost of truck	$60,000
Lifespan	6 years
Residual value	$10,000
Net cost of truck	$50,000

Now incorporate the JPL *Equipment Costing Formula* into this calculation as shown in Fig. 9.13.

FIG. 9.13 JPL EQUIMENT COSTING FORMULA (TRUE COST OF A 4X4 VEHICLE-WINTER USE ONLY)

$$\frac{\$50,000}{(\text{Lifespan} \div 2) \times \text{usage}}$$

$$= \frac{\$50,000}{(6 \div 2) \times 10 \text{ hours} \times 50 \text{ visits} *}$$

$$= \frac{\$50,000}{3 \times 500}$$

$$= \frac{\$50,000}{1,500}$$

$$= \$33.34 \text{ per hour}$$

---

[59] Assumes the cost of the vehicle, taxes and financing charges. This example shows the cost of this vehicle as if it were only used for snow removal.

9.13 COST AND RETURN ON INVESTMENT (4X4 TRUCK - SUMMER AND WINTER USE)

A 4x4 vehicle used all year round adds another component to the equation. The vehicle is considered as equipment and is rented out on a per hour basis. Take a look at Fig. 9.14.

FIG. 9.14 TRUE COST OF A 4X4 VEHICLE[60] (4X4 TRUCK-SUMMER AND WINTER USE)	
Gross cost of truck	$60,000
Lifespan	6 years
Residual value	$10,000
Net cost of truck	$50,000

Now put the cost of the vehicle into the *JPL Equipment Costing Formula* as shown in Fig. 9.15.

FIG. 9.15 JPL EQUIPMENT COSTING FORMULA (4X4 TRUCK - SUMMER AND WINTER USE)

$$\frac{\$50,000}{(\text{Lifespan} \div 2) \text{ x usage}}$$

$$= \frac{\$50,000}{(6 \div 2) \text{ x } 10 \text{ hours x } 250 \text{ visits}^{61}}$$

$$= \frac{\$50,000}{3 \text{ x } 2,500}$$

$$= \frac{\$50,000}{7,500}$$

$$= \$6.67 \text{ per hour}$$

---

[60] Assumes the cost of the vehicle, taxes and financing charges
[61] Includes salting trips, as well as use 5 days a week, 10 hours per day, during the summer.

Fig. 9.14 assumes the cost of the vehicle, taxes and financing charges.

Fig. 9.15 includes salting trips, as well as use 5 days a week, 10 hours per day, during the summer.

9.14 COST AND RETURN ON INVESTMENT (SALTER)

The salter on the truck is also rented out as equipment. Look at Fig. 9.16.

FIG. 9.16 TRUE COST OF A SALTER	
Gross cost	$9,500
Lifespan	4 years
Residual value	$1,500
Net cost of salter	$8,000

Again, put the cost of the salter into the *JPL Equipment Costing Formula* as shown in Fig. 9.17.

FIG. 9.17 JPL EQUIPMENT COSTING FORMULA (TRUE COST OF A SALTER)

$$\frac{\mathbf{\$8,000}}{(\textbf{Lifespan} \div \textbf{2}) \; \textbf{x usage}}$$

$$= \frac{\$8,000}{(4 \div 2) \text{ x 10 hours x 50 visits}}$$

$$= \frac{\$5,000}{2 \text{ x } 500}$$

$$= \frac{\$8,000}{1,000}$$

$$= \$8.00 \text{ per hour}$$

Fig. 9.18 shows a summary of costs.

Hourly driver costs, rentals and snow removal equipment charges have been added to Cost of Goods Sold.

FIG. 9.18 SUMMARY OF COSTS

Driver Hourly Wage	$25.00
Employee Benefits 20%	$5.00
Vehicle ROI	$6.67
Snow Blade ROI	$5.00
Salter ROI	$8.00

9.15 CALCULATING FOR DOWNTIME

If downtime is not included in the 15-minute segment, then you need to back up and add downtime as follows:

- Take the hourly rate at $25 plus payroll tax of 20% or $5 and add the downtime.
- If downtime works out to 2 hours per 10 hour day, then your worker cost is now $37.50 per hour as shown below.

$$\frac{\$25 + \$5}{100\% - 20\% \text{ downtime}}$$

$$= \frac{\$30}{80\%}$$

$$= \$37.50 \text{ per hour}$$

9.16 CALCULATING BREAK-EVEN FORMULA

To obtain the break-even point for the hourly rate to do snow removal, calculate as shown in Fig. 9.19.

FIG. 9.19 BREAK-EVEN POINT FOR HOURLY SNOW REMOVAL RATE

CALCULATING TO DETERMINE HOURLY RATE (BREAK-EVEN)

$$\frac{\text{Labor} + (\$37.50)\ \text{Vehicle} (\$6.67) + \text{Blade} (\$5.00) + \text{Salter} (\$8.00)}{100\% - 42\%\ \text{overhead}}$$

$$= \frac{\$57.17}{58\%}$$

$$= \$98.57 \text{ per hour}$$

Break-even charge per hour
= $98.57 per hour (Including overhead)

9.17 CALCULATING FOR PROFIT

To obtain a profit of 20%, calculate as shown in Fig. 9.20.

FIG. 9.20 CALCULATING FOR PROFIT

$$\frac{\text{Break-even charge per hour}}{100\% - 20\%\ \text{profit}}$$

$$= \frac{\$98.57}{80\%}$$

$$= \$123.21 \text{ per hour}$$

We now have the charge rate for snow and salting on a per hour charge, not including salt.

9.18 CALCULATING FOR SALT

The cost of the salt is $80 per ton. Use the *JPL Break-Even Formula* to calculate the break-even charge per ton as shown in Fig. 9.21. To calculate for 20% profit on salt look at Fig. 9.22.

FIG. 9.21 CALCULATING FOR SALT (BREAK-EVEN)

$$\frac{\text{Cost of Goods Sold}}{100\% - \text{overhead }\%}$$

$$= \frac{\$80.00 \text{ per ton}}{100\% - 42\%}$$

$$= \frac{\$80.00 \text{ per ton}}{58\%}$$

$$= \$137.93 \text{ per ton}[62]$$

FIG. 9.22 CALCULATING FOR PROFIT (SALT)

To calculate 20% profit:

$$= \frac{\$137.93}{100\% - 20\%}$$

$$= \frac{\$137.93}{80\%}$$

$$= \$172.41 \text{ per ton}$$

---

[62] Your break-even charge per ton is $137.93. This is just for salt.

9.19 CALCULATING FOR SALTING PER TIME

If you can spread a ton of salt in 15 minutes, calculate your price for salting per time as shown in Fig. 9.23.

- To calculate the charge to the customer for spreading one ton of salt at break-even, take the $137.93 amount for the salt, add labour, which includes downtime, at $37.50.
- Add: vehicle $6.67 per hour, blade $5, salter $8).
- Divide into 15-minute segments.
- Cost for labour, vehicles, and equipment is then: $14.30 plus $20 for the salt, for a total of $59.14. This is break-even pricing.

Remember that when you calculate sixty minutes to spread one ton of salt, *downtime is included,* i.e. loading, driving from one site to another and cleaning the vehicle at the end of the day.

FIG. 9.23 PER TIME COSTS

ITEM	AMOUNT	DIVIDE BY 15-MINUTE SEGMENTS	BREAK-EVEN CHARGE ADD OVERHEAD
SALT	$80.00	$20.00	$34.48
ADDITIONAL COSTS:			
Labour	$37.50	$9.38	
Vehicle	$ 6.67	$1.67	
Blade	$ 5.00	$1.25	
Salter	$ 8.00	$2.00	
	$57.17	$14.30	$24.66
TOTAL BREAK-EVEN CHARGE			$59.14

9.20 SNOW REMOVAL BENCHMARKS

The benchmarks given in this section apply to the snow removal industry.

FIG. 9.24 SNOW REMOVAL BENCHMARKS	
Truck	$60,000
Plow	$10,000
Salter	$10,000
Total Equipment	$80,000
Lifespan	6 years
Residual (Truck, plow, salter)	$20,000

FIG. 9.25 EMPLOYEE COSTS PER HOUR

Calculate as follows:

$$\frac{\textbf{Employee cost of \$25 + \$5 benefits}}{\textbf{100 – 42\%}}$$

$$= \frac{\textbf{\$30}}{\textbf{58\%}}$$

$$= \textbf{\$51.72 break-even}$$

FIG. 9.26 EQUIPMENT COSTS PER HOUR

In this case, the truck is used for twelve months[63]. Calculate as follows:

$$\frac{\$60,000\ (\text{Truck})}{(6\ \text{years} \div 2)\text{x}\ (\text{snow removal 20 times x 10 hours}) + (\text{landscape} = 5\ \text{days x 35 weeks x 10 hours})}$$

$$= \frac{\$60,000\ (\text{less residual}\ \$10,000)}{(6\ \text{years} \div 2)\ \text{x}\ 1,950\ \text{Hrs}}$$

$$= \frac{\$50,000}{3\ \text{x}\ 1950}$$

$$= \frac{\$50,000}{5,850}$$

$$= \$8.55\ \text{per hour}$$

FIG. 9.27 PLOW AND SALTER

$$\frac{\$20,000\ (\text{less residual}\ \$0.00\ )}{(6\ \text{years} \div 2)\ \text{x}\ 20\ \text{times x}\ 10\ \text{hours}}$$

$$= \frac{\$20,000}{3\ \text{x}\ 200}$$

$$= \frac{\$20,000}{600}$$

$$= \$33.34\ \text{per hour}$$

---

[63] For landscaping, usage would be 5 days by 35 weeks by 10 hours.

FIG. 9.28 TRIAXLE TRUCK

$160,000 (Less residual $10,000)

$$= \frac{\$150{,}000}{(8 \text{ years} \div 2) \times (52 \text{ weeks} \times 5 \text{ days} \times 10)}$$

$$= \frac{\$150{,}000}{4 \times 2{,}600 \text{ hrs per year}}$$

$$= \frac{\$150{,}000}{10{,}400}$$

$$= \$14.42$$

BREAK-EVEN RATE PER HOUR

Labour $37.50 per hour + Truck $14.42 per hour

$$= \frac{\$51.92}{58\%}$$

$$= \$89.52 \text{ per hour}$$

P R I C E , $ E L L ,   P R O D U C E   …   C A N   Y O U   D I G   I T ?

● ● ●

135

FIG. 9.29 TRIAXLE TRUCK WITH HEAVY DUTY PLOW AND SALTER

$$\frac{\$40,000 \; - \; (\text{Residual } \$0.00)}{(8 \text{ years} \div 2) \; x \; (20 \text{ times } x \; 10 \text{ hours each time})}$$

$$= \frac{\$40,000}{4 \; x \; 200}$$

$$= \$50 \text{ per hour}$$

BREAK-EVEN RATE PER HOUR

Labour $37.50 + Truck $14.42 + Salter/Plow $50

$$= \frac{\$101.92}{58\%}$$

$$= \$175.72 \text{ per hour}$$

FIG. 9.30 TRACTOR WITH SNOWBLOWER

$$\frac{\$60,000 \text{ (Less residual } \$10,000\text{)}}{(10 \text{ years} \div 2) \text{ x } (20 \text{ times x } 10 \text{ hours each time})}$$

$$= \frac{\$50,000}{5 \text{ x } 200}$$

$$= \frac{\$50,000}{1,000}$$

$$= \$50.00$$

BREAK-EVEN

Labour $37.50 + Tractor $50.00

$$= \frac{\$87.50}{58\%}$$

$$= \$150.86 \text{ per hour}$$

FIG. 9.31 3-6YD LOADER[64]

$120,000 (less residual $20,000)

$$= \frac{\$100,000}{(10 \text{ years} \div 2) \text{ x } (20 \text{ times x 10 hours each time})}$$

$$= \frac{\$100,000}{\$1,000}$$

$$= \$100 \text{ per hour}$$

BREAK-EVEN RATE PER HOUR

OVERHEAD RECOVERY
Benchmark = 42% overhead

$$\frac{\text{Labour } \$37.50 \; + \; \text{Loader } \$100.00}{\text{Overhead } 100\% - 42\%}$$

$$\frac{\$137.50}{\text{Overhead } 58\%}$$

$$\$237.07 \text{ per Hour}$$

20% PROFIT

$$= \frac{\$237.07}{100\% - 20\%}$$

$$= \frac{\$237.07}{80\%}$$

$$= \$296.34$$

---

[64] Note that this type of equipment is generally used in commercial work. Salting would be an extra charge. This loader is not expensed as a cost of overhead, but is treated as if the company were renting back to the company.

In Fig. 9.31 note that:

- The 3 yd loader must now be charged out at $296.34 per hour.
- This type of equipment is usually used in commercial work.
- Salting is extra.
- This loader is not expensed as a cost of overhead, but is treated as if the company were renting back to the company.

9.20 SUBCONTRACTORS AND HOW TO CHARGE FOR THEM

The benchmark for labour is 42% of sales. This takes wages, payroll tax and downtime into consideration. For example, if you pay a person $25 per hour to do your snow work, then payroll taxes are 16.25%. Therefore the hourly wage is $29.06.

Downtime is considerably higher for snow removal than it is for lawn maintenance. Benchmark for lawn maintenance is 20%. For snow removal and/or salting it can run as high as 40%.

Downtime consists of getting the truck ready, loading it with salt, travel time to and between jobs, travel back to the shop, washing the truck and cleaning up. Therefore if it is 40% (or four hours of a ten hour day), then the hourly wage becomes $48.43 per hour.

Look at the calculation below:

$$\frac{\$29.06}{(100\% - 40\%\ \textbf{downtime})}$$

Now, benchmark overhead is 42%. Therefore, the hourly rate including downtime is divided by your overhead. This brings it to $83.51 per hour.

$$\frac{\$48.43}{(100\% - \textbf{your overhead of }42\%)}$$

Of course this is break-even pricing, and who really wants to work for break-even? Most companies try to make a 25% profit.

To do this we take break-even of $83.51 and divide this by our desired profit of 25%. The charge-out price becomes $111.35 per hour:

$$\frac{\$100.22}{(100\% \text{ desired profit of } 25\%)}$$

Labour in this case is 43.5% of the sale of $111.35 per hour. That is just snow removal. The labour rate drops when you send the same person out to do salt as the material is marked up as well to cover overhead. In other words, a larger sale with the same labour.

Perhaps if subcontractors quoted with more accuracy then these rates would be theirs. In any case, a company hiring a subcontractor at a rate of $111.35 per hour will try to make 25 points on them, or more.

This means the subcontractor is invoiced out at $111.35 ÷ 75%.

$$\frac{\$111.35}{(100\% \text{ desired markup of } 25\%)}$$

or $148.47 per hour.

The key is understanding just how difficult it can be to mark up subcontractor prices, when overhead is already in their price.

P R I C E , $ E L L ,   P R O D U C E   …   C A N   Y O U   D I G   I T ?

● ● ●
140

9.21 SUMMARY

Now we are able to determine the exact cost of doing snow removal. We have demonstrated that:

- Many companies have the possibility of lowering their overhead if they can generate the work for the machinery at the price they need.
- In order to do tender work, you need the right equipment as well as a low overhead.
- It is possible to make money in snow removal. However, it is very hard to do this with 4x4 vehicles.

This exercise has shown how overhead allows you to establish your break-even pricing, per day, per event and per hour. Though companies vary in how they handle snow and salt operations, type of equipment, vehicles and subcontractor considerations, all companies need to focus on productivity and reducing downtime. I can prove to you exactly what you need to charge, however, just because it is mathematically correct does not mean you should accept it as the final price. You need to be able to compete and deliver what the market will *bare!*

CHAPTER 10

MAKING EQUIPMENT PROFITABLE BY REDUCING LABOUR

10.1 TRADING UP CAN LOWER COSTS

There is no doubt that today arborists are better equipped and more qualified than ever before. The same can be said for most service sector businesses. Better equipment has considerably opened up the market to greater productivity and higher profits. Similarly, the number of equipment companies offering leading technology has also expanded.

While improved capacity in equipment is good news, it can also be confusing for the purchaser. A company owner may simply be overwhelmed by the choices of wood chippers and their wide range of capacity.

Most tree care business owners would probably say that they would have purchased the very best wood chipper available if money were no object, but like most of us today, they had to adjust their desires to the size of their bank accounts and/or borrowing capacity.

This chapter will illustrate some critical points to consider before purchasing any equipment.

10.2 WHAT IS THE BEST BUY?

The process of purchasing a chipper should be as logical as purchasing a chainsaw. You owe it to your financial health to purchase the right piece of equipment. Otherwise, the savings gained by purchasing the cheaper version will cost you extra wages and downtime in the long run.

As smart companies constantly seek out methods to improve productivity and thereby lower their costs of doing business, contractors must also be alert to cost-cutting methods.

The greatest expense facing the company owner is labour and employee downtime. These two costs alone can sometimes surge to 40% of every dollar of revenue. For this reason, it is critical that your employees have the most productive chipper possible.

For example, an employee *can* use a 12-inch chainsaw to cut a 24-inch diameter tree. Yes, the job will get done. But it will take four times longer to cut the tree, and the life span of the chainsaw may be just long enough to cut down that tree.

LABOUR **+** EMPLOYEE DOWNTIME **=** up to 40% of every dollar revenue

How do you calculate whether trading up to a larger, more expensive chipper is for you? What will trading up save you in costs?[65] Perhaps this chapter can give you enough mathematical information to help you zero in on the best buy for your circumstances.

---

[65] The decision to trade up is always up to the business owner. No one can tell you how to operate your tree care company, but the correct information can help you to make better purchasing decisions.

10.3 THREE TYPES OF CHIPPERS

We will look at three different types and sizes of chippers. Remember, no two chippers are alike, and each has something different to offer.

We will examine their outstanding features to determine if trading up is in your best interests, and we will look at three different sizes using industry ratios. These may or may not be applicable to you, and there may be variances pertaining to chipping hardwood as opposed to softwood.

FIG. 10.1 TYPES OF CHIPPERS				
CHIPPER SIZE (INCHES)	SPEED (FPM)	HP	COST	LIFE SPAN IN YEARS
6	100	25	$12,500 [66]	15
12	100 x 2 passes	80	$25,000 [67]	15
18	100 x 3 passes	80	$32,000 [68]	15

10.4 MACHINE COST PER HOUR

Using the JPL Machine Cost Formula, we will determine the cost per hour for each of these machines.

$$\frac{\text{Cost of machine}}{(\text{Lifespan of chipper} \div 2) \text{ x hours of use per year}}$$

Let us assume that each machine would have variable hours of use per year. If we traded up to a larger capacity machine, in effect we would be increasing productivity, as we could accomplish more work in less time.

---

[66] Hand fed.
[67] Requires feed tractor ($12,500) to feed chipper.
[68] Can pass twice as much material as the 6-inch chipper. Requires feed tractor ($12,500).

However, it would be necessary to double or triple sales to have the equal number of hours of use per year to keep that larger chipper working at peak efficiency. The cost per hour for a 6-inch chipper is calculated as shown in Fig. 10.2.

FIG. 10.2 COST PER HOUR FOR 6-INCH CHIPPER

$$\frac{\textbf{Cost of machine}}{\textbf{(Lifespan of chipper} \div \textbf{2) x hours of use per year}}$$

$$= \frac{\$12,500}{(15 \text{ years} \div 2) \text{ x } 1,200 \text{ hrs}}$$

$$= \frac{\$12,500}{9,000}$$

$$= \$1.39 \text{ per hour}$$

The cost per hour of a 12-inch chipper is calculated as shown in Fig. 10.3.

FIG. 10.3 COST PER HOUR FOR 12-INCH CHIPPER

$$\frac{\textbf{Cost of machine}}{\textbf{(Life-span of chipper} \div \textbf{2) x hours of use per year}[69]}$$

$$= \frac{\$25,000 + \$12,500 \text{ feed tractor}}{(15 \text{ years} \div 2) \text{ x } 750 \text{ hours}}$$

$$= \frac{\$37,500}{5,625}$$

$$= \$6.67$$

---

[69] Because we upgraded to a faster, more powerful machine, it was necessary to feed the chipper by tractor with an attached grapple. Due to the increased productivity, the hours of use will decrease dramatically, provided net sales remain approximately the same. Note the difference between 1,200 hours on the 6-inch chipper versus the 750 hours on the 12-inch chipper.

The cost per hour of an 18-inch chipper is calculated as shown in Fig. 10.4

FIG. 10.4 COST PER HOUR FOR 12-INCH CHIPPER

$$\frac{\textbf{Cost of machine}}{\textbf{(Lifespan of chipper} \div \textbf{2) x hours of use per year}}$$

$$= \frac{\$32{,}000 + \$12{,}500 \text{ feed tractor}}{(15 \text{ years} \div 2) \text{ x } 500 \text{ hours } ^{70}}$$

$$= \frac{\$44{,}500}{3{,}750}$$

$$= \$11.87$$

For many tree care company owners, this would be the end of the story, as it is obvious that the 6-inch chipper costs a lot less per hour. Look at Fig. 10.5.

FIG. 10.5 COST PER HOUR FOR EACH CHIPPER

TYPE OF CHIPPER	$ COST PER HOUR
6-inch chipper	1.39
12-inch chipper	6.67
18-inch chipper	11.87

---

[70] The 18-inch chipper is almost three times as productive as the 6-inch chipper. Here again, with a more productive machine and without a corresponding increase in sales, we can expect to put fewer hours on this machine than the 6-inch chipper.

10.5 COST PER EMPLOYEE HOUR

While the costs listed above reflect real expenses, the story is just getting interesting. To date, there are no chippers that can operate entirely by themselves. An operator is required to get the show on the road.

We will assume that two workers are required to feed each chipper. While different crews may use very different methods for feeding their chippers, for the purposes of this exercise, I have allowed for two workers per machine.

We have established the cost of the machine per hour, but we have to factor in the cost per worker hour to arrive at the real cost of the chipper. For simplicity's sake, let us say that we would pay the same rate per employee hour regardless of whether the upgrade would be to a 12-inch chipper or 18-inch chipper.

We will assume that you pay $15.00 per hour per employee to feed a 6-inch chipper, and it take these two employees two hours to dispose of the trees and brush at a job site. In other words, the total cost to dispose of this debris with different chippers would be as follows.

Look at Fig. 10.6 to 10.8.

FIG. 10.6 COST TO DISPOSE DEBRIS WITH 6-INCH CHIPPER		
HOURS	**COST**	**TOTAL**
2 hours of 6-inch chipper machine time	2 x $1.39	$2.78
4 worker hours @ $15.00 per hour	4 x $15.00	$60.00
TOTAL COST		**$62.78**

If we would upgrade to a 12-inch chipper, we would be able to perform twice the work, but another piece of equipment would be required to feed the chipper.

The two-hour job performed by the 6-inch chipper will now take less than one hour, give or take a few minutes. Look at Fig. 10.7.

FIG. 10.7 COST TO DISPOSE DEBRIS WITH 12-INCH CHIPPER		
HOURS	**COST**	**TOTAL**
1 hour of 12-inch chipper machine time	1 x $6.67	$6.67
2 worker hours @ $15 per hour	$30.00	$30.00
TOTAL COST		**$36.67**

Now we will examine the 18-inch chipper, which has the capacity to perform approximately three times the work of a 6-inch chipper.

The two-hour job performed by the 6-inch chipper will now take less than 40 minutes, give or take a few minutes. See Fig.10.8.

FIG. 10.8 COST TO DISPOSE DEBRIS WITH 18-INCH CHIPPER		
HOURS	**COST**	**TOTAL**
18-inch chipper: $11.87 x 40 minutes	$7.91	$7.91
2 workers @ $15.00 per hour x 40 minutes	$20.00	$20.00
TOTAL COST		**$27.91**

We can see on an apples-to apples comparison that the 18-inch chipper costs the least to operate. See Fig. 10.9

FIG. 10.9 OPERATOR COSTS FOR ALL CHIPPERS	
CHIPPER TYPE	**COST**
18-inch	27.91
12-inch	36.67
6-inch	62.78

10.6 OTHER COSTS TO CONSIDER

Business would be simple if there were only operator costs and machine costs to total. However, every business also has overhead to consider and these costs must also be taken into account.

Once we calculate the total cost of doing business, we can establish how much we need to charge the customer. This is where the real differences show up. To calculate how much to charge the customer, we will use the JPL Estimating Formula. To establish break-even:

$$\frac{\text{Cost of Goods Sold}}{100\% - \text{Overhead }\%}$$

We have already calculated the important "cost of goods sold" figures (the cost of the machine per hour and the employee cost per hour), but some important and expensive elements are not yet included.

Missing from the cost calculations are the following. [71]

1. *Federal and state/provincial payroll taxes* will inflate *the per hour cost* in each example accordingly. These taxes vary greatly from one company to another.
2. *Overhead costs* can vary greatly, depending on the size of the company.
3. *Employee Downtime:* which can rise as high as 25%, depending on the travel time involved with each job.

---

[71] It is beyond the scope of this chapter to examine these variable costs, but you can insert them yourself within the cost of goods sold to arrive at final figures for your specific situation.

Generally, large companies have an average overhead of 25% and small companies average over 40%.

We will use the 40% overhead in these examples, as the vast majority of companies have overhead expenses ranging closer to that figure.

We now have all the information required to use the JPL Estimating Formula to establish our break-even point (no desired profit), and we will determine how low we are prepared to price the job.

LARGER COMPANIES = **25% average overhead**

SMALLER COMPANIES = **40% average overhead**

10.7 WHAT TO CHARGE THE CUSTOMER

For the 6-inch chipper, calculate as shown in Fig. 10.10.

FIG. 10.10 CALCULATING BREAK-EVEN POINT

$$\frac{\text{Cost of Goods Sold}}{100\% - \text{Overhead } \%}$$

$$\frac{\$62.78}{100\% - 40\%}$$

$$= \frac{\$62.78}{60\%}$$

$$= \$104.63 \text{ for the job}$$

As discussed previously, to do the two-hour job with two workers using the 6-inch chipper, you would charge $104.63.

This would pay your two workers $15 per hour for two hours each.

It would also pay for the hourly charge of the 6-inch chipper, and it would pay your 40% overhead expense. However, there would be no profit on this job.

To establish a 10% profit, calculate as follows:

FIG. 10.11 CALCULATING FOR 10% PROFIT (6-INCH CHIPPER)

$$\frac{\text{Break-even}}{100\% - 10\%}$$

$$= \frac{\$104.63}{90\%}$$

$$= \$116.26$$

For the 12-inch chipper, calculate as follows for the break-even point to the customer.

Insert the charge per hour that was calculated previously ($26.67) and apply it to the formula as shown in Fig. 10.12.

FIG. 10.12 CALCULATING BREAK-EVEN POINT (12-INCH CHIPPER)

$$\frac{\text{Cost of Goods Sold}}{100\% - \text{Overhead }\%}$$

$$= \frac{\$36.67}{100\% - 40\%}$$

$$= \frac{\$36.67}{60\%}$$

$$= \$61.12 \text{ for the job}$$

It is interesting to note that, though the job is identical, you can now charge your customer $61.12 if you have the 12-inch chipper.

The amount includes paying both workers $15 per hour, and they can complete this job in one hour instead of two.

You can cover the cost per hour of the more expensive machine and the additional tractor with a much lower price. Remember, there is no profit added to this number.

To calculate a 10% profit, look at Fig. 10.13.

FIG. 10.13 CALCULATING FOR 10% PROFIT (12-INCH CHIPPER)

$$\frac{\text{Break-even}}{100\% - 10\%}$$

$$= \frac{\$61.12}{90\%}$$

$$= \$67.91 \text{ for the job}$$

Finally, we will use the JPL Estimating Formula to establish how low we are prepared to price the job with the 18-inch chipper. For break-even point, look at Fig. 10.14.

FIG. 10.14 CALCULATING BREAK-EVEN POINT (18-INCH CHIPPER)

$$\frac{\text{Cost of Goods Sold}}{100\% - \text{Overhead }\%}$$

$$= \$27.91$$

$$(100\% - 40\%)$$

$$= \frac{\$27.91}{60\%}$$

$$= \$46.52 \text{ for the job}$$

P R I C E , $ E L L , P R O D U C E … C A N Y O U D I G I T ?

• • •

153

So, if you had the 18-inch chipper, you could do the exact same job in 40 minutes, pay both workers, and cover the cost of the most expensive machine, as well as your overhead expense.

For a 10% profit, calculate as shown in Fig. 10.15.

FIG. 10.15 CALCULATING FOR 10% PROFIT (18-INCH CHIPPER)

$$\frac{\text{Break-even}}{100\% - 10\%}$$

$$= \frac{\$46.52}{90\%}$$

$$= \$51.69 \text{ for the job}$$

Please note that the examples given are best-case scenarios and do not include many costs, such as interest paid to finance these machines, employee downtime and state/provincial or federal payroll taxes.

However, all other costs related to the chipper, such as gas, insurance and maintenance are included in overhead expenses.

The intention of this chapter is to provide mathematical information to help you make smarter decisions. You can add your own personal information and customize the formula to gain a different perspective on productivity.

The right piece of equipment and/or vehicle will reduce labour costs. Reducing labour costs, allows for more sales, jobs, productivity and profits.

Pay close attention to the type of equipment you purchase. Chapter 11 discusses the selection of equipment.

What works best for the job?

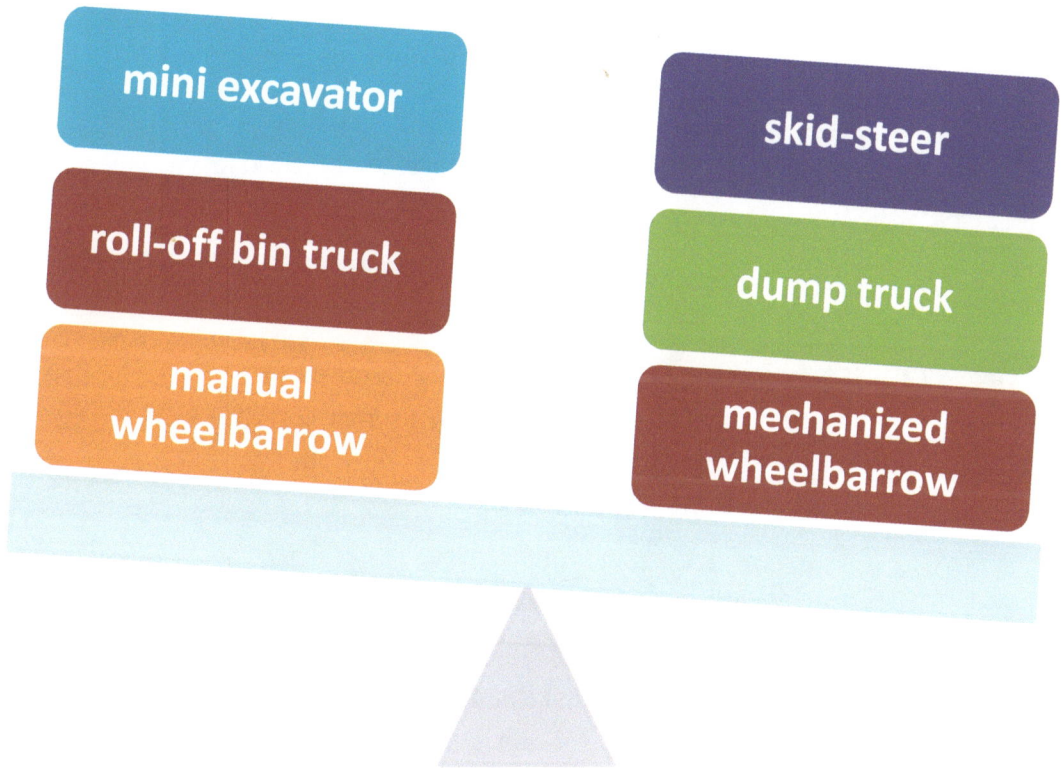

mini excavator

skid-steer

roll-off bin truck

dump truck

manual wheelbarrow

mechanized wheelbarrow

CHAPTER 11

SELECTING THE RIGHT EQUIPMENT: COST IS NOT THE ONLY ISSUE

11.1 MATCHING EQUIPMENT TO THE JOB

There are certain inescapable criteria for purchasing the right equipment. First, the equipment must match the job for which it is intended. This sounds easy enough. However, since no jobs are identical this is easier said than done.

You can simplify the selection process by talking to your equipment dealer. A qualified dealer should be knowledgeable in all the specifications about lawn mowing equipment and can help to direct you in making the correct choice for your needs.

Most dealers today are highly trained, service-oriented and backed by the manufacturer.

You can be sure that their reputation is based on recommendations. Otherwise, they would not have survived in business.

The wide assortment of equipment is very confusing to most contractors. Many contractors deal with their confusion by just walking into a dealership, quickly looking over the equipment on the floor before asking, *Is this the cheapest machine you have available?*

11.2 ASKING THE RIGHT QUESTIONS

Some people have difficulty in asking the right questions, perhaps because they have a fear of appearing foolish. When they find out later that they purchased the wrong equipment, it is an affront to their sense of pride or superior technological expertise.

They may try to cover up their error by blaming the dealer.

Their reasoning goes something like this: *If the machine I bought was not the best for me, then why was it available for sale?* In fact, they should have asked the dealer this question: *Which of your machines best suits my needs?*

11.3 CAN YOU AFFORD IT?

The purpose of this chapter is to help you find the right piece of equipment by asking the right questions. The focus here is on the decision-making process from a job bidding perspective.

The first question you should ask yourself before purchasing anything should always be: *Can I afford it?* In this case, we are not asking if you have the money, but what happens to your charge-out rate when you purchase a particular piece of equipment.

You should always take into account any potential increase in productivity that could result from buying a superior machine. This is especially important when the machine lowers the per hour cost for your job.

Will the more expensive machine increase productivity? Ask yourself these questions:

- Can I charge adequately for the equipment?
- Can I get a return on investment?
- Can I still be competitive?
- Can I increase productivity?

To answer these questions, you will have to obtain certain information from your equipment dealer:

- Cost of the machine.
- Life expectancy of the machine in hours.
- Operating capacity of the machine.

You also need to look at certain figures pertaining to your own company, such as:

- Your company's overhead as a percentage of sales.
- Hourly rate of pay for the equipment operator.
- Per year usage hours of the machine.

From this information, you can figure out how much you need to charge per hour. Is this rate competitive? This rate determines if you can afford the machine.

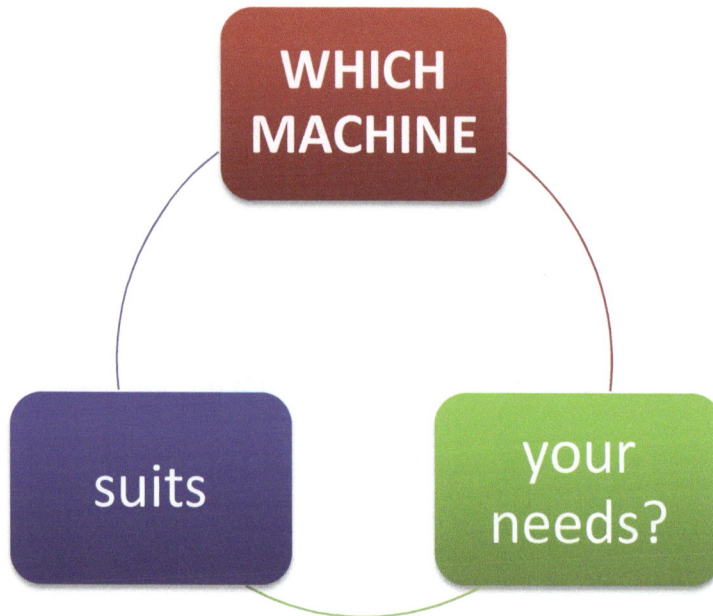

P R I C E , $ E L L ,   P R O D U C E   …   C A N   Y O U   D I G   I T ?

• • •

158

11.4 COMPARING TWO TYPES OF LAWN MOWERS (A CASE STUDY)

Accurate Maintenance maintains lawns for condominiums. This company is looking for a machine to cut grass for properties of three acres and up in size. Aiming for the "manicured look," *Accurate Maintenance* provides not only the lawn cutting services but the collection of lawn cuttings and debris as well.

What are the options for *Accurate Maintenance*?

1. A hydrostatic "walk behind" machine that cuts 48" wide and bags at the same time. The price tag for this machine is $7,000.
2. A 3-wheel 48" "riding tractor" that not only cuts and mulches but vacuums all cuttings and debris. Another feature of this type of machine is an implement that de-thatches the lawn and picks up mulch. This machine costs $18,000 or about three times as much as the former.

Many contractors today are trying to reduce their debt load as much as possible, and for this reason would be inclined to choose the first machine and save the second machine for a "maybe next time" possibility.

Accurate Maintenance decided to ask the equipment dealer for assistance. The following is an excerpt of a conversation with a salesperson who understands the industry.

SALESPERSON: Maybe I can show you how the riding tractor would be a better choice for you. Can you tell me a little about your company?

ACCURATE MAINTENANCE: Sure, I can see you would rather sell us the $18,000 machine.

SALESPERSON: Well, I would rather have you make the best decision for your needs. I'd like to help out any way I can. Why don't we take a look? Just how many hours of use do you have for these machines?

ACCURATE MAINTENANCE: I guess I would need a machine for 25 hours per week for 30 weeks.

SALESPERSON: In other words, you would use the machine 750 hours a year? At that rate, the machine would have a lifespan of approximately four years.

ACCURATE MAINTENANCE: That seems about right.

SALESPERSON: How much would you pay your operator if we include payroll burden?

ACCURATE MAINTENANCE: With taxes, insurances, and WSIB premiums, I guess it adds up to $18 per hour.

SALESPERSON: Do you know what your overhead costs are in relation to your sales?

ACCURATE MAINTENANCE: Not off the top of my head.

SALESPERSON: That's OK. For calculation purposes, we will just use the average overhead for a company of your size.

ACCURATE MAINTENANCE: I have three crews and I handle about $250,000 in sales.

SALESPERSON: OK. According to a report I have, the average overhead for a company with your sales range is 40%. A benchmark company of your size could have an overhead percentage equal to 32% of sales, with increased efficiencies.

We will use 40% as our overhead figure. For you to attain 32% overhead, this would require better productivity per crew. For instance, a crew of three can actually attain $175,000 of gross sales per truck.

- We now have all the required information so that we can use the JPL Estimating Formula to calculate what you should be charging your customer per hour.

- Let's look at your cost per employee including downtime. Your cost for the operator is actually $15 plus the payroll burden of 20%. This brings the cost per employee to $18 per hour.

- If you cannot charge your customers for downtime, travel time, coffee breaks and time for sharpening blades, you should incorporate at least 20% extra in your hourly charge to compensate yourself.[72]

SALESPERSON: This way your employee is actually costing you $22.50. (Look at Fig. 11.1).

FIG. 11.1 EMPLOYEE COST

$$\frac{\$18 \text{ per hour}}{100\% - 20\% \text{ downtime}}$$

$$= \frac{\$18}{80\%}$$

$$= \$22.50 \text{ per hour}$$

ACCURATE MAINTENANCE: That's about what I figured. What about the machine?

---

[72] Downtime can vary from company to company. It really depends on the job. The average company loses 2 hours in downtime per 10 hour day. This is a major concern as companies today try to lower downtime while increasing productivity.

SALESPERSON: To calculate the hourly cost for the $18,000 machine, we will use the JPL Equipment Costing formula and calculate as follows. (Look at Fig. 11.2).

FIG. 11.2 COST OF $18,000 MACHINE

$$\frac{\text{COST OF MACHINE}}{(\text{Lifespan} \div 2) \text{ x yearly usage in hours}}$$

$$= \frac{\$18,000}{(4 \text{ years} \div 2) \text{ x } 750 \text{ hours}}$$

$$= \frac{\$18,000}{1,500 \text{ hours}}$$

$$= \$12.00 \text{ per hour}$$

In other words, the $18,000 machine costs you $12 per hour to use. Based on what you have told me about the usage of your machine, you will earn $36,000 over a four-year period, (4 years x 750 hours x $12).

You are actually earning "return on investment."

$18,000 MACHINE = $12 per hour cost

Let's have a look at what happens when you buy the $7,000 machine. To figure out the hourly cost for the $7,000 machine, we would calculate as follows. (Look at Fig. 11.3).

FIG. 11.3 COST OF $7,000 MACHINE

$$\frac{\text{Cost of machine}}{(\text{Lifespan} \div 2) \text{ x yearly usage in hours}}$$

$$= \frac{\$7,000}{(3 \text{ years} \div 2) \text{ x } 750 \text{ hours}}$$

$$= \frac{\$7,000}{1,125 \text{ hours}}$$

$$= \$6.22 \text{ per hour}$$

Therefore, the $7,000 machine costs you $6.22 per hour. As you can see, it is possible to earn "return on investment" with both machines.

ACCURATE MAINTENANCE: Great. Can you also tell me how much I would have to charge my customer per hour?

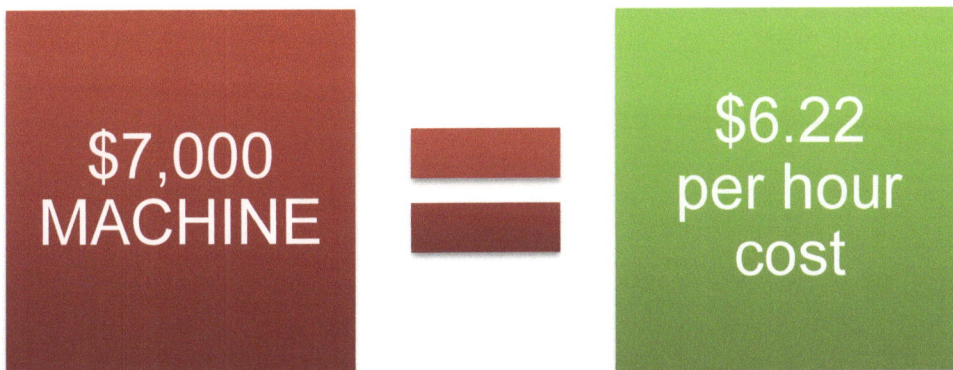

$7,000 MACHINE = $6.22 per hour cost

SALESPERSON: Well, we now have all your costs. We can continue with the JPL Estimating Formula to figure what you should be charging. Let us look at the $18,000 machine first.

To figure out the hourly (break-even charge), calculate as follows. (Look at Fig. 11.4).

FIG. 11.4 HOURLY BREAK-EVEN CHARGE

$$\frac{\text{The operator at } \$22.50/\text{hour} + \text{the equipment at } \$12.00/\text{hour}}{100\% - \text{your overhead of } 40\%}$$

$$= \frac{\$22.50 + \$12.00}{100\% - 40\%}$$

$$= \frac{\$34.50}{60\%}$$

$$= \$57.50 \text{ per hour for break-even}$$

ACCURATE MAINTENANCE: You are giving me a break-even price at $57.50 per hour. Where is my profit?

SALESPERSON: Correct. To get 10% profit, you will have to charge out at $63.89 per hour. (Look at Fig. 11.5).

FIG. 11.5 FOR 10% PROFIT

$$\frac{\$57.50 \text{ Break} - \text{even}}{100\% - 10\% \text{ profit}}$$

$$= \frac{\$57.50}{90\%}$$

$$= \$63.89 \text{ per hour}$$

ACCURATE MAINTENANCE: Wow, I can't charge out at $63.89 per hour. Should I buy the $3,000 machine?

SALESPERSON: Maybe I should tell you one more thing before you make your decision.

ACCURATE MAINTENANCE: What's that?

SALESPERSON: Since the $18,000 machine not only cuts and mulches but also picks up all cuttings and debris, it eliminates the extra hours you would need for raking up and passing the leaf and grass blower. How much time would that save you?

ACCURATE MAINTENANCE: I'm not sure.

SALESPERSON: Suppose you have a three-acre maintenance job that requires cutting and raking. A three-acre job using the $18,000 machine will cut this lawn in less than two hours and bag it in three hours.

The $7,000 walk behind with the same 48" deck will cut and bag the same property in five hours.

In fact, both machines are actually rated to cut quickly under optimum conditions. At 80% of speed and at 5 mph the $18,000 machine can cut 1.9 acres per hour.

Based on what we have learned so far, using the $18,000 machine would mean charging $57.50 per hour to break even and $63.89 per hour for a 10% profit. However, you can do the same job twice as fast with the $18,000 machine.

CONTRACTOR: How much would I have to charge for the $7,000 machine?

SALESPERSON: Same formula, except the equipment costs you $6.22 per hour instead of $12. Therefore, to figure out the hourly charge for the $7,000 machine calculate as follows. (Look at Fig. 11.5).

FIG. 11.5 HOURLY CHARGE FOR $7,000 MACHINE

$$\frac{\$22.50 \text{ employee cost/hour} + \$6.22 \text{ machine cost/hour}}{100\% - 40\% \text{ Overhead}}$$

$$= \frac{\$28.72}{60\%}$$

$$= \$47.87 \text{ for break-even}$$

For a 10% profit, calculate as follows:

$$= \frac{\$47.87}{100\% - 10\%}$$

$$= \frac{\$47.87}{90\%}$$

$$= \$53.19 \text{ per hour}$$

So what is the better buy?[73]

Perhaps we should summarize the performance of the two machines:

---

[73] Look at the "Acres per hour efficiency" chart (Fig. 11.6). Note that two productivity ratings are shown, one at 100% and one at 80% efficiency. Many manufacturers use 100% efficiency ratings for sale purposes. Exmark believes an 80% efficiency rating is more representative of actual mowing conditions as it allows for turns and overlapping.

P R I C E , $ E L L ,   P R O D U C E   …   C A N   Y O U   D I G   I T ?

• • •

166

- The $18,000 machine is able to cut and clean three acres in three hours at $63.89 per hour for a $191.67 charge to your customer.
- The $63.89 per hour charge earns you a 10% profit and covers downtime and return on investment, as well as paying your employee benefits.
- The $7,000 "walk-behind" cuts and cleans the same three acres in six hours.
- At $53.19 per hour, you would need to charge your customer 6 hours x $53.19 or $319.14.

SALESPERSON: Now, which machine better suits your needs?

ACCURATE MAINTENANCE: Hard to believe, but it looks like you have shown me in black and white that the $18,000 is obviously the better buy in my particular case.

Find a machine → that suits your needs

FIG. 11.6 ACRES PER HOUR EFFICIENCY

ACRES PER HOUR PRODUCTIVITY— EFFICIENCY AT 100% AND 80%*

MPH	32" 100%	32" 80%	36" 100%	36" 80%	44" 100%	44" 80%	48" 100%	48" 80%	52" 100%	52" 80%	60" 100%	60" 80%
1.5	.48	.39	.55	.44	.67	.53	.73	.58	.79	.63	.91	.73
2.0	.65	.52	.73	.58	.89	.71	.97	.78	1.05	.84	1.21	.97
2.5	.81	.65	.91	.73	1.11	.89	1.21	.97	1.31	1.05	1.52	1.21
3.0	.97	.78	1.09	87	1.33	1.07	1.45	1.16	1.58	1.26	1.82	1.45
3.5	1.13	.57	1.27	1.02	1.56	1.24	1.70	1.36	1.84	1.47	2.12	1.70
4.0	1.29	1.03	1.45	1.16	1.78	1.42	1.94	1.55	2.10	1.68	2.42	1.94
5.0	1.62	1.29	1.82	1.45	2.22	1.78	2.42	1.94	2.63	2.10	3.03	2.42
6.0	1.94	1.55	2.18	1.75	2.67	2.13	2.91	2.33	3.15	2.52	3.64	2.91

CHAPTER 12

A LESSON ON DEPRECIATION:
DOES YOUR EQUIPMENT PAY YOU BACK?

12. 1 WHAT'S WRONG WITH THIS PICTURE?

Let's make a deal. You lend me $10,000 for one year, and at the end of the year, I will give you back $10,000. Is it a deal? Of course not! Obviously, you want and expect a return on your money. But if you don't think the exchange I've proposed is a good deal, why are you doing just that when it comes to your equipment and vehicles?

Many service companies purchase capital equipment and then seem perfectly content to watch that equipment depreciate in value by 30% each year. A normal cost of business, you might say. Not getting a return on your investment has somehow become acceptable. But smart cost analysis and proper bidding can help reduce this financial burden.

Let's examine what typically happens when you buy a truck. Suppose you paid $40,000 for it in 2010. One year later, it was worth $28,000, assuming a depreciation expense of 30% ($12,000).

As shown in Fig. 12.1 your depreciation after eight years is $37,694.08. Your truck retains a residual value of $2,305.92 and if you think you will actually get that amount when you try to sell it in 2017, good luck.

FIG. 12.1 DEPRECIATION TABLE ($40,000 TRUCK AT 30% A YEAR FOR 8 YEARS)

YEAR	VALUE	DEPRECIATION	RESIDUAL VALUE
2010	40,000.00	12,000.00	28,000.00
2011	28,000.00	8,400.00	19,600.00
2012	19,600.00	5,880.00	13,720.00
2013	13,720.00	4,116.00	9,604.00
2014	9,604.00	2,881.20	6,722.80
2015	6,722.80	2,016.84	4,705.96
2016	4,705.96	1,411.79	3,294.17
2017	3,294.17	988.25	2,305.92

TOTAL DEPRECIATION $37,694.08

12.2 SHORTCHANGING YOUR COMPANY

We can see from Fig. 12.1 that after eight years, your investment of $40,000 is returned to you as an expense of $37,694.08 and $2,305.92 in residual value. Some investment!

The problem with depreciation is that by following the income tax regulations and using depreciation as an expense in your budget, you are only accounting for the direct cost of the equipment or vehicle.

This gives you a false picture of your true costs. Therefore, you are shortchanging yourself when it comes to getting a return on your equipment or vehicle investment.

What's wrong with this picture? Let's go back to the offer I made. Didn't you expect something in return for the $10,000 I wanted to borrow from you? So why do you think it is okay to invest $40,000 in a truck and get almost nothing in return for that investment?

12.3 EATING YOUR EQUITY

You may claim your "return on investment" (ROI) is hidden in the profit you made last year. Unfortunately, I know what you pay yourself,[74] and I also see your profits. It's a sad fact that most service business owners would make more money working for someone else.

Not only do many of you pay yourselves less than you pay your workers, but you are actually eating your equity, due to the decreasing value of your equipment each year, especially if you do not charge for ROI. Consequently, each year you manage to stay in business, your net worth diminishes. This is reflected in "retained earnings" on your income statement.

The problem is magnified if you are over-equipped and unable to charge a fair price to cover the true cost of this equipment, including the cost of your money. Each year, the total value of all your equipment and vehicles decreases. What do you have to show for it?

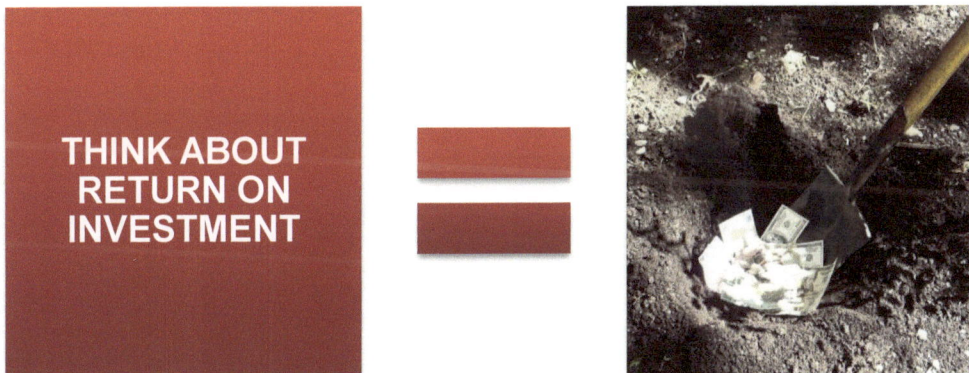

At this point, you are probably asking yourself, "How much of a return should I expect?" Simply put, a good return on investment (ROI) means that when your $40,000 truck goes to the vehicle scrap yard, you have enough money to

---

[74] And in some cases, how little you compensate your employees.

replace it with comparable equipment. That's money in real cash, not just the ability to borrow more cash.

If this still isn't making sense, ask those old-timers[75] in the trade why they always paid *cash* for their equipment. Most of these people never had a charge card or a line of credit at the bank. Ever wonder why? Loans are expensive, and that's why those old-timers avoided them. Perhaps the banks considered them a financial risk as well.

The answer to this dilemma is simple, at least in theory. You must charge your customers enough for your vehicle on every job so that you get back every penny you paid over the vehicle's eight-year lifespan, plus a return on your investment.

Keep in mind that some vehicles and equipment will not last eight years and others may last longer.

FIG. 12.2 INVESTMENT TABLE:

PERFORMANCE OF A $40,000 INVESTMENT EARNING 5 % COMPOUND INTEREST[76]

YEAR	$ INVESTMENT	$ INTEREST	$ YEAR-END TOTALS
1	40,000.00	2,000.00	42,000.00
2	42,000.00	2,100.00	44,100.00
3	44,100.00	2,205.00	46,305.00
4	46,305.00	2,315.25	48,620.25
5	48,620.25	2431.01	51,051.26
6	51,051.26	2552.56	53,603.82
7	53,603.82	2,680.09	56,284.01
8	56,284.01	2,814.20	59,098.21

TOTAL INTEREST[77]   **19,098.21**

---

[75] Try asking your parents this question.
[76] 5% interest can be earned through mortgage lending, which is somewhat higher than savings or investment funds.
[77] Compounded interest is paid monthly and therefore this figure would be higher.

If this sounds outrageous, have another look at the Investment Table (Fig. 12.2). Suppose that, instead of buying the vehicle, you invested your $40,000 in a mortgage earning 5% interest.[78]

Note that even if you charge an hourly rate that completely covers the cost of the vehicle, you are still not giving yourself an adequate return on investment.

At the end of eight years, you would have earned a total of $19,098.21 in interest and still have your initial $40,000 intact. This is your return on investment. Certainly, this is a very safe way to earn interest. Obviously, the more risk you take in investing, the more you should earn.

I always find it interesting that the people who claim it is difficult to get a return on the money they invest for vehicles and equipment are the same people who do not seem to mind paying for their equipment with a 48-month loan.[79]

If, once the loan is paid off, they would continue to deposit the same amount every month into a separate bank account for the four-year balance of the vehicle's life,[80] they would have a return on investment as well as the cash to pay for a new vehicle.

12.4 CHARGE ENOUGH BY THE HOUR TO COVER ALL COSTS

The secret to getting a good return lies in the way you charge customers for equipment. There are three formulas you can use to calculate how much to charge:

- Formula #1: Guess
- Formula #2: Unit Pricing
- Formula #3: Charge enough by the hour to cover your costs while building a nest egg (return on investment) for new equipment.

---

[78] This is not as easy now as it used to be, but it is still possible.
[79] Or more, as the industry has now extended this period to 72 months.
[80] Provided it lasts 8 years.

FORMULA #1

Too many service companies use Formula #1. If you are guessing your costs, what you don't know *will* hurt you. Is it any wonder that so many companies continue to tell me they are busy, but they are not happy with the money they are making? Or that they seem to be working harder to make less money.

The key to a lean overhead is making equipment/vehicle(s) last for their projected lifespan. Paying proper attention to driving, operation and maintenance should allow equipment/vehicle(s) to last eight years or more.

Maintenance costs (usually 1% of sales) must be included. For a $500,000 company this would amount to $5,000 per year for eight years.

FORMULA #2

This method is easy and does serve a purpose. Basically, unit pricing consists of finding out what your competitors charge per hour and following that. So, if the going rate is $80 per hour with an operator, you simply adopt that. It makes life simpler, but do you have an *accurate* rate that applies to *your* company?

FORMULA #3

Using formula #2 is an improvement, but it's likely to yield an unsatisfactory return, since most people who do this use inaccurate numbers to cover equipment costs through general overhead and hope they get enough hours at $80 per hour. They use depreciation as an expense, *which is not accurate for budgeting*.

That's why I recommend Formula #3. This formula enables you to charge by the hour for what the equipment really costs. Knowing your exact cost per hour for that equipment helps you determine whether you should be buying, renting or subcontracting.[81]

Contractors often buy equipment based on price and do not take lifespan and productivity into account. This is a big mistake. Even if you charge an hourly rate that completely covers your costs, i.e. the price of the vehicle, loan

---

[81] Keep in mind that in this case, with formula #3, we are taking this machine out of overhead and charging it back to the company on a per diem basis.

interest, gas, taxes, licence fees, maintenance and everything else that goes into running a machine, you are still not giving yourself an adequate return on investment. So how do you take that final step?

Look at Fig.12.3 and then read the following dialogue based on a conversation I had with a contractor recently. It illustrates what needs to be considered when purchasing equipment.

FIG. 12.3 EQUIPMENT COST FORMULA

$$\frac{\text{Cost of equipment}}{(\text{Lifespan} \div \text{Return On Investment}) \times \text{Usage in hours per year}}$$

$$= \frac{\$75,000}{(8 \text{ years} \div 2) \times 900 \text{ hours per year}[82]}$$

$$= \frac{\$75,000}{3,600}$$

$$\$20.83 \text{ per hour}$$

WHEN PURCHASING A VEHICLE THINK ABOUT:

PRODUCTIVITY

LIFESPAN

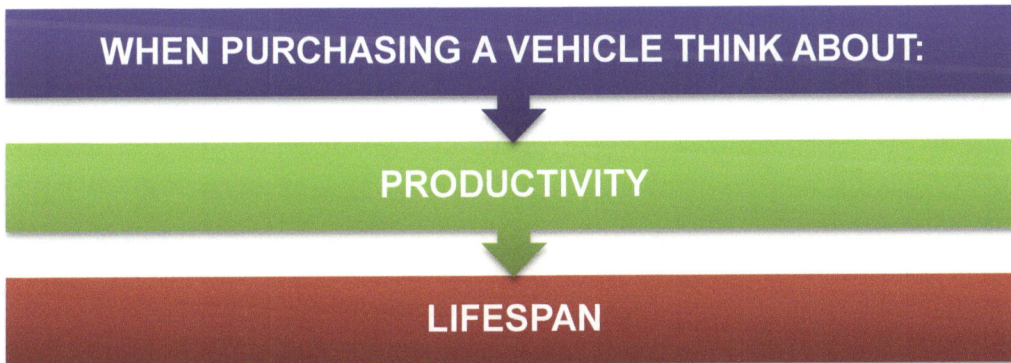

[82] Calculation is based on 6 chargeable (2 hours of downtime per day) hours per day x 5 days per week x 30 weeks.

12.4 DIALOGUE WITH A CONTRACTOR (A CASE STUDY)

CONTRACTOR: I just bought a backhoe, and I don't know what to charge for it.

ME: How much did you pay?

CONTRACTOR: $60,000.

ME: Do you need a trailer for this equipment? If so, how much will it cost?

CONTRACTOR: About $10,000.

ME: Taxes included?

CONTRACTOR: Yes.

ME: Did you pay cash, or did you finance this purchase?

CONTRACTOR: I financed it. Who has that much money?

ME: So how much did you really pay?

CONTRACTOR: $90,000. That's $60,000 for the backhoe, $10,000 for the trailer and $20,000 for the financing.

ME: How long do you think this equipment will last?

CONTRACTOR: I expect to get about eight years[83] out of it if the work stays the same.

ME: How many hours per year will that be?

CONTRACTOR: Hard to say, exactly. But I'm sure we'll use it at least 900 hours per year. That's based on 30 weeks with three 10-hour days[84] of work per week for the backhoe.

ME: Let's put all this information down on paper to see how much the backhoe will really cost your company.

---

[83] Each year the contractor needs to re-examine equipment usage to see if the expected lifespan will remain the same.

[84] When a piece of equipment goes to a job and remains there for the entire day (regardless of hourly use) it is considered a 10-hour charge to the job. The fact that the equipment is on the job site all day is considered usage on the job. The machine may only be used as little as one hour, but is charged for a full day unless it leaves the job site. This is exactly how it works when you rent from an outside source. You pay for the day, regardless of how long it is used. Downtime is not calculated.

First, I figured out how much the equipment would cost the contractor to run on a per-hour basis, including a return on investment that would allow him to buy a new truck after eight years.

To figure out the true cost of the backhoe, we first establish the cost ($90,000) and then deduct the residual value, or the amount that it will sell for in eight years. For our purposes, we will say that we can sell it for $15,000 eight years from now.

Then I divided the total cost of the equipment ($90,000 - $15,000 = $75,000) by the result of the following calculation:

(Lifespan ÷ return on investment) x usage in hours per year.

The backhoe will last for eight years, but the contractor wants to have all the expenses paid for in half that time, so the money earned by the equipment in the remaining years can build a fund for a new backhoe.

In essence, he is looking to pay for the backhoe by the time only half its life is over, so he divides the lifespan by a factor of 2.

Look at the following formula:

8 years ÷ 2 = 4 x 900 hours per year = 3,600.[85]

To pay for the cost of the backhoe, trailer and financing in four years, the contractor needs to charge as follows. Look at Fig. 12.4.

---

[85] Expressed in dollar terms, the contractor is trying to spread $75,000 in costs over 3,600 hours of work.

FIG. 12.4 CHARGING FOR THE BACKHOE

- 8 years ÷ 2 = 4
- Multiplied by 900 hours per year = 3,600
- Expressed in dollar terms, the contractor is trying to spread $75,000 in costs over 3,600 hours of work.
- To pay for the cost of the backhoe, trailer and financing in four years, he needs to charge $20.83 an hour. ($75,000 ÷ 3,600)

BREAK-EVEN POINT CALCULATION (*back to my conversation with the contractor*)

ME: Now, obviously the equipment needs gas to operate. There are also other overhead costs, as well as the labour cost for an operator. Can you tell me what your overhead expense is as a percentage of sales?

CONTRACTOR: 27.5 % of sales.

ME: We already know the cost of the truck on a per-hour basis. And notice that we did not include depreciation in our numbers. Can you tell me what you will be paying your operator, including payroll taxes?

CONTRACTOR: The operator gets $16 per hour, and payroll taxes are an additional 20%.

ME: Good. Now we can figure exactly how much you must charge per hour for this backhoe to break even.

I then started plugging the numbers into my favourite estimating formula.

The break-even point equals the total costs divided by the result of the following equation. Look at Fig. 12.5.

In this case, our total costs are $40.03 an hour. That includes the $20.83 we just calculated to pay for the equipment, loan and return on investment, the $16 the contractor is going to pay his operator and $3.20 in payroll taxes.

The contractor told me his standard overhead percentage is 27.5%. We are only doing a break-even analysis at this point.

- 100% - (27.5%) equals 72.5%.
- Divide the total costs of $40.03 an hour by 72.5% (or 0.725)
- The result is $55.21.

FIG. 12.5 BREAK-EVEN FORMULA (FOR EQUIPMENT AND OPERATOR)

$$= \frac{\text{CGS (Cost of Goods Sold)}}{100\% - \text{Overhead \%}}$$

$$= \frac{\$20.83/\text{hr for backhoe} + (\$16/\text{hr for operator} + \$3.20 \text{ for payroll taxes})[86]}{100\% - 27.5\% (\text{overhead})}$$

$$= \frac{\$40.03}{72.5\%}$$

$$= \$55.21 \text{ per hour (break-even point)}$$

ME: Do you think you can charge $55.21 per hour in your area for backhoe services?

CONTRACTOR: No sweat.

ME: Keep in mind that there is no allowance in these numbers for downtime, travel time or profit. If you do not work the machine 900 hours a year, you are going to come up short.

Still, if you are able to charge $55.21 per hour, you are at least accomplishing the following:

---

[86] Downtime is not calculated.

1. Paying your operator and all payroll taxes.
2. Covering your overhead (which includes the owner's salary and all other expenses, as well as the truck to transport the trailer and backhoe.
3. Getting a return on your investment.

CONTRACTOR: A return on my investment? Go over that again.

ME: Remember, you needed to charge the customer $20.83 per hour for use of the machine, based on 900 hours of work per year for eight years.

- If you multiply $20.83 per hour by 900 hours x eight years, the total is $149,976.
- Out of this amount, you paid $60,000 for the backhoe, $10,000 for the trailer and $20,000 for the financing.
- This adds up to $90,000, less the expected residual of $15,000 after eight years of use, which means you paid out $75,000.

12.5 GETTING RETURN ON INVESTMENT (SUMMARY)

- $149,976 less $75,000 in costs leaves you with $74,976. That is called ROI (Return on Investment).
- After eight years, you have $74,976 of ROI plus the $15,000 residual value from either selling or trading in the machine and trailer.
- This should be enough to purchase a new machine with cash. This makes you more competitive and profitable, as you are not giving $20,000 to the bank.

FIG. 12.6 RESIDUAL VALUE

- If after eight years, you can sell the trailer and backhoe for $15,000, then this must be calculated into the true cost of the machine.
- In other words, $90,000 less $15,000 residual value = $75,000.

12.6 RETAINED EARNINGS

What is the moral of this little tale? The supply of contracting services far exceeds demand in many markets. Most contractors are over-equipped and forced to eat their equity to survive. It is difficult to get a return on investment if you are bidding at a level that does not even allow you to earn a minimal profit. You may survive like this for a while, but you can only go backward for so long.

There is no simple solution to the current competitive situation, but it is evident that, if you had charged for "return on investment" when the demand for work exceeded the supply, you would have extra funds available today to help you through these difficult times.

Those funds are called "retained earnings," and they are possible only when you keep a close eye on your budget. You may want to keep this in mind when you bid on your next job.

12.7 OTHER OPTIONS

Sometimes having every piece of equipment and/or vehicle is not the answer.

Examine the ROI tables closely as well as the formulas for break-even pricing in this chapter. There are many contractors who can provide backhoe and other services for your company, i.e. as a subcontractor. Engaging the services of a subcontractor may prove to be wiser in the long run.[87]

---

[87] You may discover that you lose less money this way and may actually start making a profit.

CHAPTER 13

HOW MORE COSTS LESS (A CASE STUDY)

13.1 CAN'T RAISE PRICES

The number one complaint from mowing contractors across the country is that they cannot raise their prices. Making a profit is almost impossible. Employees are working to their limit, and overhead is about as "lean and mean" as you can get.

Contractors who are managing to make a profit[88] attribute this profit to using the right mower. When the time comes to purchase a new mower for contractors who have not yet made the quantum leap to high-productivity mowers, the equipment dealer is approached with a little dread and much apprehension, and very little cash on hand.

Without profit, it is almost impossible to make plans for that elusive day when you want to buy that high-productivity mower.

13.2 LOWEST PRICE IS NOT EVERYTHING

No matter how often we are told that this mower will last longer, go faster, cut better and save money, we always have a problem with *the price,* but the "lowest price" does not take everything into account for the financial picture.

As a matter of fact, our fixation on *lowest price* is often the cause of a poor profit picture and a troubling cash flow. Remember, the expense of that high-productivity mower must be examined carefully in conjunction with the reduction of labour expense and downtime savings.

The past five years have meant sink or swim to many contractors. It seems as though there are just too many contractors out there. As in many other

---

[88] This profit figure may still be quite small.

sectors, there is just too much supply and not enough demand. Asking higher prices is difficult; profits are not materializing, and cash flow is eroding.

We will look at mowers from a different angle: *the productivity factor.* Let me share with you a process that I use to determine which mower is the best dollar value and *not just a lower price.*

13.3 THE CHOICES

I need a new mower, and I am looking at three different mowers that I think will do the job for me. At this point in time, I have about 1,000 acres of grass to cut each year, or 33 acres per week for 30 weeks.

The mower I now use operates for four days per week and cuts eight acres per day. There are no restrictions on the sites, such as gates to block accesses, and most of the sites are a half-acre or more.

There are three possible machines that could be used to do this work:

1. A 36" *residential riding mower* priced at $3,000. This is the same type of mower I am now using and is just about all I can afford according to my budget.

2. A 36" *commercial walk behind mower* priced at $6,000. The mower which I have determined is better built and will cause me less downtime. But there's that cash flow problem, because the payments will increase my overhead, and I would have to finance the purchase.

3. A 48" *commercial riding tractor* is the mower I would really love to have. Of course I'd have to win the lottery for that one, priced at $9,000.

13.2 DOLLAR VALUE

How do these mowers measure up in dollar value? Here's the data for each mower. Take a look at Fig. 13.1 and carefully examine the data[89] for each mower.

FIG.13.1 PRICE COMPARISON

MOWER TYPE	CUTTING WIDTH	PRICE $	MPH	MINUTES PER ACRE
Residential Riding Mower	36"	$3,000	4	50
Commercial Walk Behind	36"	$6,000	6	34
Commercial Riding Tractor	48"	$9,000	6	25

Since mower capacity is usually closer to 80%, I use the following formula to calculate how many acres per hour are possible.

FORMULA FOR CALCULATING ACRES PER HOUR

$$\text{(MPH x width of cut)} \div 120 = \text{acres per hour}$$

Therefore, for the 36" riding mower, I would multiply the miles per hour (MPH) which is 4 by the width of the cut (36") and divide by 120.

$$(4 \times 36) \div 120 = 1.20 \text{ acres per hour}$$

---

[89] I have found that mowers do not operate at 100% capacity. Usually capacity is closer to 80%.

Now I divide minutes (60 for one hour) by 1.20 to get 50 minutes. As you can see in Fig. 13.1, the $3,000 mower takes 50 minutes to cut an acre versus 25 minutes for the 48" mower. I need to know the cost of each mower per hour so that I can help determine which is the best mower for the job. To determine the cost of the mower, you have to know the following:

1. The cost of the mower (including the financing costs)
2. The lifespan of the mower in years
3. Hours of use per year

EQUIPMENT COST FORMULA

<u>Total $ Cost of Equipment</u>
(Lifespan of Equipment in years ÷ 2) x (Hours of Use per Year)

FIG. 13.2 COST OF EQUIPMENT HOUR BASED ON 1000 ACRES PER YEAR

$3,000 MOWER	$6,000 MOWER	$9,000 MOWER
(3 years ÷ 2) x (834 hours)	(4 hours ÷2) x (567 hours)	(6 years ÷ 2) x (417 hours)
Cost = $2.40 hour	Cost = $5.30 per hour	Cost = $7.18 per hour

Note how the $3,000 mower costs only $2.40 per hour versus the 48" mower at $7.18 per hour. If the purchase decision was to be made strictly on *mower cost per hour,* I can assure you that I would be buying the $3,000 mower. Note also that in all cases of comparison the equipment cost per hour includes return on investment.

13.3 COST OF EQUIPMENT PER HOUR

I incorporate "return on investment" in this formula. This is important so that over the lifespan of the mower, not only will I have money from my hourly charge to pay for the mower, but I will also have funds available to buy the eventual replacement mower in the future.

By dividing the expected lifespan of the mower by 2, you automatically build in return on investment.

We will use the $3,000 mower as an example. The dealer told me that if I use this mower for 834 hours to cut 1,000 acres each year, he would recommend that I trade it in after two years, and if I take care of it, it might last three years. The mower I have right now has lasted three years.

You can see in Fig. 13.2 that the cost per equipment hour for the $3,000 mower is $2.40. If I use this mower for 834 hours for 3 years at $2.40 per hour, I will have collected $6,000.

In other words:

834 hours x 3 x $2.40 = $6,000

This is $3,000 more than I paid for the mower. This extra $3,000 plus the residual value of the mower upon trade-in time should cover the cost of a similar replacement mower.

13.4 EMPLOYEE COST PER HOUR

What about employee cost per hour? Obviously, someone is going to have to drive this mower. I pay $12 per hour for my employees to operate my mowers. I also pay payroll taxes, so that my payroll burden is 20% or an additional $2.40 per hour. Look at the formula below.

($12 per hour x 20% payroll tax)

My total employee cost per hour is therefore $14.40.

13.5 DOWNTIME COSTS

Downtime, or the time spent loading and unloading trucks, traveling to and from the job site and two coffee breaks per day add up to 20% of the workday or 2 hours of each 10-hour day. Who pays for this down time?

Of course, I must consider that I can only charge my customers for *productive time*.[90]

Therefore, to determine the real cost of my employee, I need to incorporate the downtime in the employee hourly rate, so that the customer actually pays for the (*unproductive*) downtime.

13.6 EMPLOYEE COST PER HOUR PER MACHINE

To determine employee cost per hour per machine, I divide the hourly pay of the employee plus the payroll burden by the percentage of downtime *less* 100%.

FIG. 13.3 DOWNTIME FORMULA

$$\frac{\$12.00 \text{ per hour } + \$2.40 \text{ payroll burden}}{100\% - 20\% \text{ down time}}$$

$$= \frac{\$14.40}{80\%}$$

$$= \$18.00$$

In other words, an employee who is paid $12 per hour actually costs me $18 per hour.

---

[90] Productive time is the time employees spend working on the customer's property.

Now, if you incorporate both employee and mower costs per hour, you will notice a substantial difference between the three mowers.

13.7 NOT AS PRODUCTIVE

Even though the $3,000 mower costs less to operate per hour in comparison to the other two mowers, it just takes too long to cut one acre. This is obvious when you look at Fig. 13.5.

Note that the $3,000 mower takes 50 minutes to cut an acre. To calculate this into hours, you divide 50 minutes by 60 minutes, which equals .83 hours.

FIG. 13.4 PRODUCTIVITY

COST PER HOUR	$3,000 MOWER	$6,000 MOWER	$9,000 MOWER
Employee Cost per Hour	$18.00 per hour	$18.00 per hour	$18.00 per hour
Cost per Mower Hour	$2.40 per hour	$5.30 per hour	$7.18 per hour
Total Cost per Hour	$20.40 per hour	$23.30 per hour	$25.18 per hour

FIG. 13.5 TOTAL COST PER ACRE

MOWER COST	$3,000 MOWER	$6,000 MOWER	$9,000 MOWER
Employee + Equipment Cost Per Hour	$20.40	$23.30	$25.18
Hours to cut one acre	0.83	0.57	0.42
Cost per acre	$16.93	$13.28	$10.58

- Even though the $3,000 mower is so much easier on my cash flow, this mower is not as productive.
- I cannot afford a $12 per hour employee on a $3,000 mower for 50 minutes per acre when compared to 25 minutes per acre for the 48" mower.

It seems incredible, but the mower that costs three times more than I can afford to pay is actually more affordable than I first realized.

13.5 WHAT DO I CHARGE MY CUSTOMER?

We will now take this argument to its conclusion, to see what I would have to charge my customers. In the final analysis, it is the customer who pays!

To determine this charge per acre, I need to use my cost per acre amount. See Fig. 13.5.

Using the JPL mathematical estimating formula, to determine break even, divide your company overhead into your costs per acre.[91]

BREAK-EVEN CHARGE RATE PER ACRE FORMULA

$$\frac{\text{Total Cost per Acre}}{100\% - \text{overhead }\%}$$

---

[91] I used a 40% overhead for this example. This seems to be the average overhead for maintenance companies across North America.

FIG. 13.6 BREAK-EVEN CHARGE RATE PER ACRE

$3,000 MOWER	$6,000 MOWER	$9,000 MOWER
$$\frac{\$16.93}{100\% - 40\% \text{ overhead}}$$	$$\frac{\$13.28}{100\% - 40\% \text{ overhead}}$$	$$\frac{\$10.58}{100\% - 40\% \text{ overhead}}$$
= $28.22	= $22.13	= $17.63

13.6 MORE PRODUCTIVE PER ACRE

Incredible as it may seem, the $9,000 mower proves to be not only more productive per acre, but does the job twice as fast, allowing for more sales!

To calculate for twenty percent profit, look at Fig. 13.7.

FIG. 13.7 TO MAKE 20% PROFIT

$3,000 MOWER	$6,000 MOWER	$9,000 MOWER
$$\frac{\$28.22}{100\% - 20\%}$$	$$\frac{\$22.13}{100\% - 20\%}$$	$$\frac{\$17.63}{100\% - 20\%}$$
$$\frac{\$28.22}{80\%}$$	$$\frac{\$22.13}{80\%}$$	$$\frac{\$17.63}{80\%}$$
= $35.28	= $27.66	= $22.04

On the 1,000 acres I cut each year, the $9,000 mower saves me $13,240 ($35.28 per acre for the $3,000 mower less $22.04 per acre for the $9,000 mower multiplied by 1,000 acres). This almost pays for the machine with is first year of savings!

Put your own figures into the blank tables at the end of this chapter, so that you can accurately establish what you should be charging your customers per acre.

This is the only way you can find out which mower can do this job for you and in a way that makes dollars *and* sense!

P R I C E , $ E L L ,   P R O D U C E   …   C A N   Y O U   D I G   I T ?

191

13.7 CHAPTER REVIEW

Here are the formulas for determining what you should be charging.

EQUIPMENT COST FORMULA

$$\frac{\text{Total \$ cost of equipment}}{(\text{lifespan of equipment in years} \div 2) \times (\text{hours of use per year})}$$

FORMULA FOR CALCULATING ACRES PER HOUR

$$\text{MPH} \times \text{width of cut} \div 120 = \text{acres per hour}$$

FORMULA FOR CALCULATING CHARGE RATE PER HOUR[92]

$$\frac{\text{Employee cost per hour} + \text{equipment cost per hour}}{100\% - (\text{overhead \%} + \text{desired profit \%})}$$

FIG.13.8 RATE PER ACRE AND COST PER HOUR

	$3,000 MOWER	$6,000 MOWER	$9,000 MOWER
FORMULA	$\dfrac{\$20.40}{100\% - 40\%}$	$\dfrac{\$23.30}{100\% - 40\%}$	$\dfrac{\$25.18}{100\% - 40\%}$
Charge rate per hour (break even)	$34.00	$38.83	$41.97
Hours to cut one acre	0.83	0.57	0.42
Charge rate per acre (break even)	$34.00 x 0.83 = $28.22	$38.83 x 0.57 = $22.13	$41.97 x 0.42 = $17.63
20% profit	$28.22 ÷ 80% = $35.28	$22.13 ÷ 80% = $27.66	$17.63 ÷ 80% = $22.04

---

[92] This is based on overhead of 40% as a percentage of sales.

Determine what you should be charging your customers. Put your own figures into the following tables, so that you can accurately establish what you should be charging your customers per acre.

FIG. 13.9 CUTTING MACHINE COST PER HOUR

	RESIDENTIAL RIDING MOWER	COMMERCIAL WALK BEHIND	COMMERCIAL TRACTOR
Cutting Width	36"	36"	48"
Price $	$3,000	$6,000	$9,000
Speed (MPH)	4	6	6
Minutes per Acre	50	34	25

FIG. 13.10 EQUIPMENT COST (BASED ON 1000 ACRES PER YEAR)

	$3,000 (3 yrs ÷ 2) x (834 hrs)	$6,000 (4 yrs ÷ 2) x (567 hrs)	$9,000 (6 yrs ÷ 2) x (417 hrs)
Cost per equipment hour	$2.40	$5.30	$7.18
Employee cost per hour	$18.00 per hour	$18.00 per hour	$18.00 per hour
Total cost per hour (machine + employee)	$20.40 per hour	$23.30 per hour	$25.18 per hour
Total cost per acre[93]	$20.40 x .83 hours = $16.93 per acre	$23.30 x .57 hours = $13.28 per acre	$25.18 x .42 hours = $10.58 per acre

---

[93] Productivity ratings for all machines are shown at 80% efficiency.

Put your own figures into these tables.

FIG. 13.11 CUTTING MACHINE COST PER HOUR			
	RESIDENTIAL RIDING MOWER	COMMERCIAL WALK BEHIND	COMMERCIAL TRACTOR
Cutting width			
Price $			
Speed (mph)			
Minutes per acre			
NOTES			

FIG. 13.12 EQUIPMENT COST (BASED ON 1000 ACRES PER YEAR)			
COST PER HOUR	EQUIPMENT COST	EQUIPMENT COST	EQUIPMENT COST
Equipment			
Employee			
Machine + employee			
Total cost per acre			
NOTES			

CHAPTER 14

PRODUCTIVITY FORMS

On the next pages, you will find sample forms that may be useful for your company.

- Telephone request for estimate
- Landscaping services work order
- Customer data and payment information
- Estimator's site report
- Daily job report and schedule
- Special services
- Maintenance sales cost analysis
- Landscaping sales cost analysis
- Call backs and replacements
- Change order
- Thank you letter to customer
- Daily job report
- Daily productivity report
- Employee productivity report
- Project management task list
- Vehicle and equipment responsibility agreement
- Product/plant purchase order
- Equipment and vehicle maintenance
- Vehicle condition report
- Equipment maintenance tasks
- Contract
- Contract (sample clauses)
- Watering instructions
- Lawn maintenance instructions
- Plant maintenance instructions
- Maintenance of interlock pavers
- Arrange for estimate
- Customer's evaluation report

TELEPHONE REQUEST FOR ESTIMATE (SAMPLE)

ORIGIN OF REQUEST: ❑ TELEPHONE ❑ WALK-IN ❑ EXHIBITION

Name of Customer ❑ Mr. ❑ Mrs. ❑ Ms.

Phone (Home):   Phone (Work):   Cell:

Best time to call: ❑ Morning   ❑ Afternoon   ❑ Evening

HOW DID YOU LEARN OF OUR COMPANY?

❑ Our customer   ❑ Ad in paper/magazine/flyer   ❑ Phone book

❑ Saw our vehicles   ❑ Exhibition   ❑ Signs on job site

❑ Referral by: Name: Address (area):

WHAT TYPE OF JOB?

❑COMMERCIAL	❑NEW HOME	❑DESIGN ONLY
❑RESIDENTIAL	❑ESTABLISHED HOME	❑MATERIAL AND INSTALLATION
❑INTERLOCK DRIVEWAY	❑INTERLOCK PATIO	❑INTERLOCK SIDEWALK
❑POOL LANDSCAPING	❑DECK	❑FENCING
❑RETAINING WALL	❑LAWN PROGRAM	❑LAWN MAINTENANCE
❑OTHER		

NOTES

RETURN CALL: SET UP APPOINTMENT FOR:

This request for estimate was handled by:

Would prefer (design/sale) work is done by:

Today's date:

LANDSCAPING SERVICES WORK ORDER (SAMPLE)

CUSTOMER:	ADDRESS:	
HOME PHONE:	OFFICE PHONE:	CELL PHONE:
EMAIL:	FAX:	BEST TIME TO CALL:
APPOINTMENT TIME: AM/PM	DESIGNER:	

SERVICES REQUESTED

❑   Consultation ($75. per hour + sales tax plus travel time at $75. per hour + sales tax)

❑   Sketch ($75. per hour + sales tax

❑   Full scale drawing. Fee to be arranged.

❑   Other (Indicate below)

HOW DID YOU LEARN OF OUR COMPANY?

❑ Our customer	❑ Ad in paper/magazine/flyer	❑ Phone book
❑ Saw our vehicles	❑ Exhibition	❑ Signs on job site
❑ Referral by:	Name:	Address (area):

NOTES

CUSTOMER DATA AND PAYMENT INFORMATION (SAMPLE)

Name of Customer ❏ Mr. ❏ Mrs. ❏ Ms.

Address:

Phone (Home):   Phone (Work):   Cell:

Best time to call: ❏ Morning ❏ Afternoon ❏ Evening

❏ **Customer has been informed that proposal is ready**   **Indicate date:**

❏ **Customer has received proposal**   **Indicate date:**

NOTES

PAYMENT INFORMATION		
TOTAL AMOUNT:	AMOUNT RECEIVED:	BALANCE DUE:
METHOD OF PAYMENT		
❏ CREDIT CARD	❏ CHEQUE	❏ CASH
❏ ON ACCOUNT	❏ MONEY ORDER	❏ PURCHASE ORDER*
*Indicate purchase order number, if applicable:		
Prepared by:		
Date:		

ESTIMATOR'S SITE REPORT (SAMPLE)

PROJECT:	DATE:

CUSTOMER:	ADDRESS:	

INDICATE BELOW AS APPLICABLE

❏compacted soil	❏soil needs aeration	❏good drainage
❏flood problems	❏rocks, brush, weed, trees	❏heavy thatch
❏normal access for equipment	❏access to water	❏lawn needs fertilization program
❏flower beds need attention	❏topsoil required	❏obstructions on job site

Type of terrain:

Open trenches or holes (describe):

Degree of slope:

Critical inspection problems:

Estimated driving time from office to job site:

NOTES

PREPARED BY:	DATE:

DAILY JOB REPORT AND SCHEDULE (SAMPLE)

JOB FUNCTION	ESTIMATED TIME	ACTUAL TIME	TOTAL HOURS	COMMENTS
CUSTOMER:		SUPERVISOR:		DATE:

SPECIAL SERVICES (SAMPLE)

PROJECT:	DATE:

CUSTOMER:	ADDRESS

INDICATE BELOW AS APPLICABLE

☐landscaping	☐do it yourself design	☐consultation
☐inspection	☐plant replacement	☐lawn repairs

DESCRIBE AREAS OF CONCERN

Watering:

Planting method:

Fertilization:

Materials:

Insect/fungus:

Damage:

Other:

Guarantee:

RECOMMENDATIONS:

PREPARED BY:	DATE:

MAINTENANCE SALES COST ANALYSIS (SAMPLE)

CUSTOMER:	ADDRESS:	
HOME PHONE:	OFFICE PHONE:	CELLPHONE:
MAILING ADDRESS (IF DIFFERENT):		
JOB START DATE:	JOB COMPLETION DATE:	

ACCOUNTING	AMOUNT	METHOD OF PAYMENT
Billing:		
Deposit:		
Balance due:		

LIST JOB COSTS BELOW

CATEGORY	COST
Evergreens	
Shrubs	
Vines	
Groundcover	
Flowers/perennials	
Hard goods	
Fertilizer	
Mulch	
Sod	
Labour	
Employee payroll taxes	
Workplace Safety Insurance Board	
Delivery charges	
Subcontracting	
Equipment rental	
Sales tax	
COST OF GOODS SOLD TOTAL	
Overhead factor	
Earnings per employee hour	
Gross profit on job	
Prepared by:	Date:

LANDSCAPING SALES COST ANALYSIS (SAMPLE)

CUSTOMER:	ADDRESS:	
HOME PHONE:	OFFICE PHONE:	CELLPHONE:
MAILING ADDRESS (IF DIFFERENT)		
JOB START DATE:	JOB COMPLETION DATE:	

ACCOUNTING	AMOUNT	METHOD OF PAYMENT
Billing:		
Deposit:		
Balance due:		

LIST JOB COSTS BELOW

CATEGORY	COST
Evergreens	
Shrubs	
Shade trees	
Groundcover	
Sod	
Hard goods non-taxable	
Hard goods taxable	
Mulch	
Other	
Labour	
Employee payroll taxes	
Workplace Safety Insurance Board	
Delivery charges	
Subcontracting	
Equipment rental	
Sales tax	
COST OF GOODS SOLD TOTAL	
Overhead factor	
Earnings per employee hour	
Gross profit on job	

Prepared by:	Date:

CALL BACKS AND REPLACEMENTS (SAMPLE)

CUSTOMER:	ADDRESS:	
HOME PHONE:	OFFICE PHONE:	CELLPHONE:
DATE OF ORIGINAL JOB:	DATE OF REPLACEMENT	INVOICE NUMBER:

REPLACEMENT MATERIAL

QUANTITY	ITEM DESCRIPTION	PRICE	TOTAL
TOTAL			

LABOUR COSTS

Number of employees:	Number of hours:	Total labour costs:

Notes:

Prepared by:	Date:

CHANGE ORDER (SAMPLE)

CUSTOMER:	ADDRESS:	
HOME PHONE:	OFFICE PHONE:	CELLPHONE:
DATE OF ORIGINAL JOB:	DATE OF REPLACEMENT	INVOICE OR P/O NUMBER:

REPLACEMENT MATERIAL (LIST ITEMS TO BE REPLACED)

QUANTITY	ITEM DESCRIPTION	PRICE	TOTAL
TOTAL			

LABOUR, EQUIPMENT AND VEHICLE CHARGES

Rate is $75 per hour plus equipment and vehicle charges plus applicable tax.

Labour	
Equipment	
Vehicle	
Tax	
Total	

Homeowner agrees to charges listed above	
Supervisor's signature	

This signed change order will now form part of your contract with Let's Landscape. The total amount for this extra work will be listed on a separate invoice. Balance owing is due upon receipt.

Let's Landscape!

Mr. And Mrs. Consumer
123 Anytown,
Anyprovince, Canada

Dear Mr. And Mrs. Consumer,

Thank you for considering our Design and Build team for a landscaping estimate. I appreciate that your business decision will be a major investment and sincerely hope that we will be able to offer you the best possible design for your home.

Thank you for considering our firm. Please call me personally if I can be of further assistance to you.

Sincerely yours,

J. Doe

Design and Build Team Manager

Let's Landscape Company

DAILY JOB REPORT (SAMPLE)

JOB NAME/NUMBER	ADDRESS:	
HOME PHONE:	OFFICE PHONE:	CELLPHONE:
DATE:	WEATHER:	SUPERVISOR:

EMPLOYEES

EMPLOYEE NAME	START TIME	FINISH	WORK PERFORMED

MATERIAL USED

QUANTITY	MATERIAL RECEIVED	MATERIAL NEEDED	TOOLS NEEDED

EQUIPMENT USED

COMPANY EQUIPMENT	RENTED EQUIPMENT	HOURS USED RATE	RATE

ADDITIONAL WORK

CUSTOMER REMARKS

PLEASE ATTACH ALL INVOICES/RECEIPTS TO THIS FORM EACH DAY

DAILY PRODUCTIVITY REPORT (SAMPLE)

CREW:

DATE:

JOB SITE	TIME IN	TIME OUT	HOURS WORKED	DOWNTIME	COMMENTS
TOTAL HOURS WORKED					
DOWNTIME TOTAL					

EQUIPMENT DESCRIPTION	PROBLEM TO BE CHECKED/REPAIRED	FOLLOW UP	DATE

EMPLOYEE PRODUCTIVITY REPORT (SAMPLE)

EMPLOYEE NAME:			UNIT NAME/NUMBER		
DATE	CLIENT NAME	TIME IN	TIMEOUT	TRAVEL TIME	EQUIPMENT USED
FUEL USED:					
EQUIPMENT USED:					
NOTES					

PROJECT MANAGEMENT TASK LIST (SAMPLE)

PROJECT	PAGE _____ OF _____
PROJECT LEADER	BACK UP
PROJECT TEAM MEMBERS	

ITEM #	TASK	TEAM MEMBER TIME ALLOTTED					COST	COMPLETION DATE
		HRS	HRS	HRS	HRS	HRS		
	TOTAL							

VEHICLE AND EQUIPMENT RESPONSIBILITY AGREEMENT (SAMPLE)	
Employee name:	Date of hiring:

❑ I have a current valid driver's license. The license number is:

❑ I do not have a current valid driver's license.

I have read and full agree to the following:

1. If permitted to operate company vehicles, I must do so in a careful and safe manner at all times and observe all traffic laws and ordinances.

2. When operating company equipment (mowers, spreaders, trimmers, etc.) I must do so in a safe manner, in accordance with manufacturers' guidelines and company policies.

3. I am responsible for maintaining the interior of company vehicles.

4. After operating company vehicles and/or equipment, I am responsible for properly securing it, in accordance with company policy, to prevent it from being lost or stolen.

5. I am responsible for up to $300 of the cost of repairing any company vehicle, equipment or property that is damaged because of my *improper operation* or my failure to obtain prescribed *preventative maintenance.*

6. I am responsible for up to $300 of the cost of replacing lost or stolen equipment due to my failure to properly secure a vehicle or piece of equipment in accordance with company policy.

7. I understand that receiving two (2) moving citations or causing two (2) accidents in any 12-month period is grounds for immediate termination.

8. I understand that when vehicles or equipment are damaged due to my negligence, carelessness or recklessness, I am also subject to disciplinary action, up to and including termination.

9. I understand that if I am found to have stolen or failed to return a company vehicle or piece of equipment which is assigned to me, I will be terminated and will not be eligible for rehire.

10. I authorize the company to withhold from monies due me any obligation created as described above in compliance with applicable law.

WITNESSED BY

Branch Manager (signature):	Date:
Employee (signature):	Date:

PRODUCT/PLANT PURCHASE ORDER (SAMPLE)

YARD			GARDEN CENTRE			
LANDSCAPE JOB SITE			DATE NEEDED		COMMENTS	

PLEASE FILL OUT PRODUCT/PLANT INFORMATION BELOW

RECEIVED	QUANTITY	SIZE	PRODUCT/PLANT	COST	SUG. RET. PRICE	SUPPLIER

Discounts available:

Transportation costs:

Issued by:	Date:
Authorization:	Date:

EQUIPMENT AND VEHICLES MAINTENANCE (SAMPLE)

EQUIPMENT	TIRES	TUNEUP	OIL CHG	BATTERY	PAINT	ENGINE	PWR TRAIN	TOTAL

VEHICLE CONDITION REPORT (SAMPLE)

VEHICLE NO.	START TIME	STARTING MILEAGE	ENDING MILEAGE	DATE

As required by safety regulations, please inspect the items listed, check if defective and describe in "remarks".

ENGINE

❏fluid leaks	❏oil level	❏coolant level
❏battery	❏transmission	❏exhaust system
❏belts and hoses	❏brake fluid	❏air brake system

INSIDE CAB

❏glass and mirrors	❏seat belts	❏gauges and horn
❏windshield wipers	❏fire extinguisher	❏safety flares or triangles
❏registration and permits	❏accident and fuel card	❏brakes
❏parking and service	❏clutch	❏fuel level
❏radio	❏first aid kit	❏engine warm up and operation
❏steering	❏cleanliness	❏interior lights
❏service due	❏other	❏other

AIR SYSTEM

❏low air warning device	❏air pressure/loss/static/max pr.	❏air leaks applied (max. 3 lbs/min)
❏adjustment needed:	❏yes	❏no
❏other	❏other	❏other

OUTSIDE

❏tires	❏wheels and lug nuts	❏reflectors
❏steering	❏fuel cap/tank/mounting	❏new body damage
❏parking lamps	❏head lamps, high/low	❏turn signals
❏brake lights	❏emergency flasher/lamps	❏back up alarm
❏cleanliness	❏tools and equipment	❏mud flaps
❏traffic cones	❏ropes and tarp	❏other

VANS

❏window latches	❏entry and exit doors	❏transport racks
❏exterior/interior	❏other	❏other

TRAILER

❏trailer coupler device	❏trailer lights	❏reflectors
❏ramps	❏tie downs	❏chain binder
❏decking	❏other	❏other

REMARKS

❏No defects found	Date:
Pre-trip driver's signature	
End of trip driver's signature	

P R I C E , $ E L L ,   P R O D U C E   …   C A N   Y O U   D I G   I T ?

• • •

214

Equipment Maintenance Tasks

DESCRIPTION OF TASK	January	February	March	April	May	June	July	August	September	October	November	December
Large Equipment:												
Lube, Oil, Safety check												
Tune-up												
Coolant Maintenance												
Transm. Maintenance												
Vehicles:												
Lube, Oil, Safety check												
Tune-up												
Coolant Maintenance												
Emissions Certification												
Clean Vehicle												
Riding Mowers Only:												
Lube, Oil, Safety check												
Tune-up												
Coolant Maintenance												
Transm. Maintenance												
Push Mowers & Edgers:												
Grease												
Check & Sharpen Blades												
Clean Filter												
Check Belts												
Clean Mower												
Adjust Mower Height												
Small Equipment:												
Tune-up, oil Change												
In Running Order												
Clean												
Safety Inspection												

(Each month is divided into columns: 1 Week, 2 Week, 3 Week, 4 Week, 5 Week)

CONTRACT (SAMPLE)

Page No.   Pages

SUBMITTED TO		PHONE	DATE
STREET		JOB NAME	
CITY, PROVINCE AND POSTAL CODE		JOB LOCATION	
ARCHITECT	DATE OF PLANS		JOB PHONE

We hereby submit specifications and estimates for:

_____

_____

_____

_____

_____

_____

_____

_____

_____

_____

We propose hereby to furnish material and labour - complete in accordance with above specifications, for the sum of:

_____dollars ($_____).

All material is guaranteed to be specified. All work to be completed in a workmanlike manner according to standard practices. Any alteration or deviation from above specifications involving extra costs will be executed only upon written orders, and will become an extra charge over and above the estimate. All agreements contingent upon strikes, accidents or delays beyond our control. Owner to carry fire, windstorm and other necessary insurance. Our workers are fully covered by Workplace Safety Insurance Board.

Signature of Homeowner_____

Note: This contract may be withdrawn by us if not accepted within _____ days.

We agree to the Terms and Conditions of Sales as stated on The CONTRACT. In consideration of the above services, we agree to pay this account on due date and further agree to pay 24% per month service charge on unpaid balance after due date.

Signature of Homeowner_____

Signature of Representative_____

DRAWINGS

If work is to be done according to drawings or blue prints, standard graphical symbols are to be used or a legend is to be marked on drawings. The contractor shall not be held responsible for errors or omissions on plans or specifications furnished by others.

PAYMENT

Should the owner bequeath or sell his property before the completion of the work in progress, the unpaid balance of the present contract will become due and immediately redeemable without summons or notice, unless the purchaser or successor assumes each and all of the conditions of the present contract.

DAMAGE BY OTHER TRADES

This contractor is not responsible for damages or delays caused by other trades.

ESCALATOR CLAUSE FOR MATERIALS AND WAGES

Prices specified concerning material and labour rates pertaining to this contract are those effective at the date of the signature of the present contract. Should the contractor be delayed in the execution of this work for reasons beyond his control, necessary adjustments could be made with regards to prices quoted in the present contract i.e., if the cost of material and/or wages increase.

INDEMNITY CLAUSE (BREACH OF CONTRACT)

In the event of annulment or breach of contract, or in the event that work is stopped or suspended for a period exceeding thirty (30) days for a reason non imputable to the contractor, an automatic indemnity of at least thirty-five per cent (35%) of the cost of the contract or of the work still to be executed will become due to the contractor; payments already disbursed being the possession of the contractor.

EQUIVALENT PRODUCTS

If it is impossible for technical reasons or others, to procure in time an item from a specific manufacturer, the contractor is, under the circumstances, hereby authorized to substitute said item by one generally known of the same worth, quality and specification.

WORK STOPPAGE

Notwithstanding any provision to the contrary, in the event that the customer should fail to make his payments within the terms of the contract the contractor could stop work or annul the contract without summons or legal notice without prejudice to his other rights or legal recourses under the terms of the present contract

RESERVE OF PROPRIETORSHIP

All appliances, materials and accessories shall remain the property of the contractor until full payment of all amounts of the contract. The customer will assume all risks pertaining to loss.

CLAUSES

It is understood that the client allows our firm to park and unload on their property to do the above-specified work. Any damage to said property will be repaired to normal at contractor's cost.
All utilities are to be supplied by the client and have been considered in the quote.

Don't forget to water

When plants are moved from the garden centre to your garden, remember, these plants have been watered and cared for on a daily basis. It is very important that you water and care for your plants in a similar fashion. Natural rainfall or two-hour sprinklings usually are not enough. You must still hand soak your plants during dry spells in April, July or November. Don't drown your plants!

- If you have a clay-type soil and drainage is very poor, you should put rocks or crushed bricks in the bottom of the planting hole. You may even have to drain water away with drain tiles to a lower spot. Water no more than once every week or 10 days, but water generously when you do.
- If you have sandy soil, don't let your plants dry out in hot weather. You should water with the hose two or three times a week. (15-20 minutes).

NEW LAWNS

- The most important ingredient is adequate water, so water once daily and twice a day from late June to late August.
- Sprinkler should be kept on for one hour per section.
- Continue watering for 10 to 14 days, unless it rains.
- The lawn may be cut after two weeks after installation date.

ESTABLISHED LAWNS

- Water on a weekly basis.
- If rain is insufficient, water at least for one hour per section, to allow for saturation of 6" depth.
- Leave grass 1 3/4" to 2" high and rake up the clippings.

LAWN MAINTENANCE

- Fertilize with a weed/feed winterizer.
- Do not use liquid fertilizers because they promote thatch and cost more, if you compare the amount of nitrogen.
- Fertilize 4 times a year.
- Use slow-release fertilizer in mid-April.
- If soil is heavy clay type, lawn should be aerated each spring.

Your plants have come from an environment where they were watered daily. They are now in the proper soil, but they will need adequate water if the roots are to develop properly.

- Adequate water means using a sprinkler system or soaker hose for up to one hour.
- Repeat this procedure on a weekly basis.
- The best time to water is in the morning (before 7 AM or earlier)

Large new trees or shrubs should be watered every second or third day for the first two weeks.

- Use about a gallon of water per tree or shrub.
- Weekly water should be sufficient after that.
- The best way to retain the water is to keep the soil circled around the tree or shrub.

Hand cultivating allows for better circulation and prevents proliferation of weeds and insects.

- If you add peat moss, mix it with the soil, because peat moss alone can harden.
- If you use bark as a mulch, remember that the decaying process requires nitrogen and will rob it from your plants. To compensate, add a little extra fertilizer.

MAINTENANCE OF INTERLOCK PAVERS (SAMPLE)

YOUR INTERLOCK DRIVEWAY OR WALKWAY

These pavers have been installed on a compacted base of gravel to allow for normal use.

Although the driveway has been constructed to handle most vehicles, we recommend keeping heavy trucks off the driveway, especially in spring when the ground is saturated with water.

To maintain your driveway or walkway, just sweep coarse sand between the joints once a year, or more frequently if you wash your car often.

Individual soiled or broken pavers can easily be changed. Styles and colours are constant.

Avoid walking along the edges of pavers. They are influenced by the surrounding wet soil.

Make your neighbours green with envy

Add beauty, shade and privacy to your yard with our energy-saving ideas and quality nursery stock. Renew your outdoor living space and impress your neighbours!

Let's Landscape can renew your environment. We provide on-site consultation, landscape design drawings, itemized estimates, quality stock and friendly service.

Arrange an appointment with one of our designers. Call the Landscape Design Department at 123-456-7890 for more information.

CUSTOMER'S EVALUATION REPORT (SAMPLE)

Providing our customers with quality service is not our only commitment to you, but the standard by which we strive to be the best in all aspects of our work. Please take a moment to fill out this evaluation report and remember that all deficiencies will be acted upon immediately to your satisfaction. Please add this report to your remittance of your monthly invoice in the pre-stamped envelope. Thank you for your comments.

CUSTOMER:	ADDRESS:	
HOME PHONE:	OFFICE PHONE:	CELL PHONE:
MAILING ADDRESS (IF DIFFERENT)		

Please indicate your level of satisfaction with our maintenance crew, our quality of work and standards of service and products.

	EXCELLENT	SATISFACTORY	NEEDS ATTENTION
THE CREW			
Appearance			
Working standards			
Manners			
THE GROUNDS			
Lawn			
Flower beds			
Shrubs			
Evergreens			
Annuals			
Edging			
Pruning			
OVERALL APPEARANCE			
Colour			
Balance			
Cleanliness			

COMMENTS

Should we contact you? ❏	When is the best time to reach you?
Date:	Would you like information on our other services? ❏

WHAT THE MARKET WILL "BARE"
An estimating manual and mathematical pricing system for service companies. By J. Paul Lamarche

COMMON $ENSE ECOLUTION
This book explores different methods you can use to create healthier gardens. By J. Paul Lamarche.

$EEDS FOR CHANGE
Perceived dollar value is the name of the game, and mass merchandisers with targeted selection and lower prices are winning that retail game. What are you going to do about it? By J. Paul Lamarche

YOU CAN'T MANAGE BY STANDING AROUND
This book will help service company managers build winning sales teams while increasing productivity.
By J. Paul Lamarche.

FRONT LINE TRAINING
Employees cannot train themselves or learn everything about customers and service on the Internet or by watching a video. You, as the IGC owner/manager, have the power to create a store with "impossible customer service" but you have to walk the talk! A solid sales training program can raise average customer sales by up to $5 per customer. The training techniques in this book will show you how to create "impossible customer service" for your store. By J. Paul Lamarche.

COMMON $ENSE TOOLS FOR IGC MANAGERS
This book will help IGC managers understand employee management principles, while demonstrating how to create opportunities for creativity in the work environment. Managers will learn to delegate, monitor and motivate from a position of respect and credibility. By J. Paul Lamarche.

PRICE, $ELL, PRODUCE ... CAN YOU DIG IT?
A benchmark overhead for a landscaping company is 32%, including ROI (return on investment for vehicles and equipment.) The reality however is quite different, as the average overhead in landscaping is about 40%. This figure is eight points above the benchmark and represents quite a substantial difference. Does this mean that landscaping companies are out on a spending spree? This is definitely not the case, based on the financial data I have examined. Almost all the companies I observed during this time seem to be suffering from this same high overhead problem. What is the reason for this high overhead? By J. Paul Lamarche.

INDEX

www.ingramcontent.com/pod-product-compliance
Lightning Source LLC
Chambersburg PA
CBHW041726210326
41598CB00008B/795